Education
for Churchmanship

Education
for Churchmanship

ROBERT S. CLEMMONS

ABINGDON PRESS
NASHVILLE   NEW YORK

EDUCATION FOR CHURCHMANSHIP

Copyright © 1966 by Abingdon Press

Library of Congress Catalog Card Number: 66-21968

SET UP, PRINTED, AND BOUND BY THE
PARTHENON PRESS, AT NASHVILLE,
TENNESSEE, UNITED STATES OF AMERICA

To DAVID
whose
love of life
illuminating smile
and fidelity of purpose
put into our domestic orbit
a swirling nebula of memories

PREFACE

Propelled by the swift pace of social change and challenged by the "knowledge explosion" of our times, the leaders of educational ministries in the Protestant churches have reconstructed their images of churchmanship, revised their educational programs, and redesigned curricula for persons across the life span. This book examines these educational developments. It seeks to clarify some of the new images of churchmanship emerging from current biblical, theological, and historical thinking as well as current psychological and social images of man, to the end that clergy and laity may understand the roles and relationships necessary in a mutual ministry. It describes some assumptions, understandings, and procedures upon which the new learning theories, the new curriculum design, and changing leadership roles are being built so that church renewal may be supported by intelligent and responsible concern. It interprets emerging understandings of the church as "gathered and scattered" and designates some specific contributions which adults can make to its life and mission.

Included in the audience for whom this book is written are the following: ministers who are aware of forces changing patterns of the church's ministry, directors of Christian education in local churches who guide the development of lay leadership, conference administrators who plan educational programs for adults, laymen who are members of commissions or boards of education making decisions that will involve the future patterns of adult education in local churches, teachers and students in seminaries and colleges who may use it as an interpretive resource for their preparation for their educational ministry, and leaders of adult groups in local churches.

Many opportunities to work closely with persons planning for a new day in Christian education as well as invitations to lecture in seminaries, universities, and colleges gave added incentive to the writing of this book. The opportunity was given to present the material in Chapter I to a class in Christian education conducted by Dr. Donald Maynard, Dr. William C. Moore, and Dr. Walter L. Holcomb at Boston University School of Theology. "What May the Churches Expect of Laymen Today?" was presented as a paper to the Consultation on Training of Laity sponsored by the General Board of Education of The Methodist Church. The material presented in Chapter IV on the meaning of churchmanship was developed during my participation in the Cooperative Curriculum Project composed of representatives of seventeen major denominations. Chapter V emerged during my four years of research and data gathering while participating in the work of the Adult Curriculum Study Committee of The Methodist Church. The substance of this chapter was delivered as a lecture to a summer audience at the Iliff School of Theology in Denver. The materials describing the experiment on leadership in Chapter VI were collected

while I was teaching at Scarritt College and were presented at
Duke Divinity School as a lecture to a Christian education class
led by Dr. W. Arthur Kale. The substance of the material for
Chapter VII was presented first at Emory University Church
and Community Workshop. The articles written for the Sep-
tember, 1964, issue of *Adult Teacher,* on "Changing Meanings
of Work" set forth some of the basic ideas in Chapter VIII.
Some of the insights concerning "Family Life—Christian Style"
were gleaned from the conversations with my wife as we worked
on the research for and later guided the discussion groups at
the National Family Life Conference. These opportunities to
serve The Methodist Church have brought to focus many of
the perceptions in this book.

For her diligence, patience, and persistence in typing and
helping me prepare the manuscript, I want to express gratefully
my appreciation to Mrs. J. W. Lauderdale.

ROBERT S. CLEMMONS

CONTENTS

PART I

Reexamining
Assumptions About the Laity

This section reexamines some of the biblical, theological, and historical assumptions that underlie the relationships of persons in the Christian community.

Chapter 1 reviews some contemporary images of churchmanship in the light of biblical perspectives currently discussed by theologians and the practical images of leadership which laymen experience as they are trained for management in the world of work. A critique of some clergy-laity roles is stated in the light of these theological and practical perspectives.

Chapter 2 reviews the current psychological and social potentials of the laity to be the church and reexamines the many roles of the laity in the light of the history of the church. Flexibility and adaptability—rather than routine and rigidity—in the matter of changing his social circumstances are clearly shown to characterize the laity. Laymen have responded in keeping with their understanding of the church in each age.

Chapter 3 seeks to clarify the six primary roles of the laity in the light of biblical and theological thinking that describes the life and mission of the church.

Chapter 1

Changing Images of Churchmanship

The most significant fact of our time is change. The farmer boy who fell asleep yesterday on the haystack dreaming that he might fly like a bird awoke today at the controls of a space ship soaring through outer space at unprecedented velocities. The laborer who longed simply for a reduction of hours in his back-breaking toil watches his bored son examine the flashing lights of an automated machine which does the work of five hundred men in less time than they could do it and with more accuracy. The African native who danced yesterday before a spirit-infested campfire hoping to drive poverty and disease from the life of his people sits today in the circle of nations voting on sending shipments of medical supplies to needy peoples of the world. The isolated mountain dweller who

waited for a weekly newspaper to come his way now finds that
the whole world is a whispering gallery and that what is happening in a remote section of Tibet is transmitted immediately
all over the globe. Change is occurring everywhere at an
accelerated rate.

THE DIMENSION OF CHANGE

Institutions which formerly had a great deal of equilibrium
are changing rapidly too. Education, which previously relied
upon the older and more mature persons to transmit the culture
to the younger ones, now finds that as much new knowledge
has been discovered in the lifetime of one person as all mankind
had discovered up to the time of this person's birth. As one
teacher put it, "These young people are asking questions that I
can't even think." This fact requires institutions of learning to
develop new programs that improve the quality, scope, and
content of learning. In science the astrophysicist has pushed
back the horizons of the heavens, the biochemist has brought
us to the brink of the creative processes of life itself, the atomic
engineers have opened the gates of the furnaces of hell in our
faces so that the survival of life depends upon profound changes
in the nature of man himself.

Likewise, churches are changing. The rapid movements of
populations—from rural regions to the city, of families with
children to the suburbs, of older adults back into the cities again
—have forced many churches to ask what is essential and what
is peripheral in the work of the church. Moreover, the increasing demands of larger and larger numbers of children and youth
and older adults, while the young adult and middle-aged population which serves them recedes, have created leadership problems that put a great strain upon the program of any active
church. As leaders become short in supply, the churches are
being forced to reassess those activities that are not in keeping
with its life and mission. Routine ways of working are being

scrutinized. "Why," people are asking, "should we continue this kind of activity? Does it enable persons to become vitally aware of their relationship to God? Amid the resurgence of thought and life around us, where can the church point to the living proof of its relevance to life?" By asking these questions church leaders are beginning to search for answers with new courage, a new desire for depth of meaning, and a new sense of relevance.

Changes in Churchmanship

Simultaneously, changes are taking place in the church's perception of styles of churchmanship. The "glamor boy" type who was the product of the success psychology of the 1920's is being weighed and found wanting, because of a lack of depth in relationships, to meet the strains of change in our time. This type of leader is passing because he is unable to help groups confront issues, make decisions, and accept the pain of responsibility. He involves fewer and fewer people, and these wait upon him to make the decisions for them. They feel less and less responsible for the work of the church. They may admire this leader for his facile way with people, but they eventually lose interest when they discover that he is basically a performer and they are spectators. This kind of relationship is not integral to life in the Christian community. It did not exist between the Master and his disciples. It is not the basic relationship between man and God. Above all, it does not describe the kind of self-denying discipleship on which the church is built. It frequently ends in the performer's breaking down under the strain of trying to out-perform himself while his followers become frozen.

A second picture of churchmanship that is being reassesssed vigorously is the "power figure" who seeks to run the church from some central office. This style of Christian existence is built primarily upon a power-dependency relationship between the person giving orders and those who take them. He is known as the man who gets things done. In his code of conduct efficiency is valued more highly than what happens to people. He uses the budget, statistics, quotas to coerce people into doing what he has preconceived that they should do. Although people may comply outwardly with his demands for a while, they feel inwardly that he is blocking their chances to develop as persons who are capable of deciding goals, changing under their own self-discipline, and accepting responsibility for achieving them. They feel their spiritual freedom to choose and appropriate personal meanings must be placed in subordination to the demands of the power figure. They may try to live their life in the church in a repressed state of passivity, resigning themselves to whatever may come. Frequently, however, they begin to view other persons as hostile and threatening.[1] They may gather others about them and challenge or attack the authority figure, whether the person is a clergyman or a layman. Thus, a church begins to polarize as these persons begin to act out in the open arena of interpersonal relations the drama of conflict taking place within themselves. What happens to persons in the midst of this conflict is of serious consequence to the church. Leadership that seeks to help persons develop toward Christian maturity is being called upon to reevaluate the power-dependency relations. This leadership is trying to find the authority for the church in the understanding by the congregation of the life and mission of the church, so they may act in ways that enable persons to embody the spirit of Christ in their relationships to others. As they do so, more laymen may assume responsibility for the witness and mission of the church in the world.

A third image of churchmanship which is being reevaluated by persons planning activities in churches is the "status figure." More persons are giving a second thought to the suggestion, "If we only had a big-name speaker, I know that meeting

[1] T. W. Adorno, The Authoritarian Personality, pp. 237-39.

would . . ." Really? What actually would happen? Since Vance Packard has pointed out the synthetic nature of status-seeking relationships, Christian persons have been probing deeply into the recognition factor as a basis for the work of the church. Does prestige rub off on the organization that is able to keep its program going by having a steady stream of status persons appear as speakers or entertainers? Or does this encourage forms of pretense which block a group from facing the real issues inherent in its own life and structure? Does it cause persons to discover the real potentialities of individuals in their own fellowship and enable them to clarify their own beliefs and understand each other better? A prestige person may bring new insights and information to a group, but the members of the group still must learn to respond to one another in honesty of speech and feeling, share their belief systems with each other, and evoke in each other a response of trust, understanding, and love.

As persons begin to reassess the styles of churchmanship operative today, they are asking some probing questions: Is churchmanship a matter of addition? Are there a number of beliefs stated propositionally or traits made visible behaviorally that make persons churchmen? Do we need to gain more biblical, theological, and historical perspective so that our image of churchmanship may reflect more accurately the life and mission of the church itself?

SOME BIBLICAL VIEWS OF CHURCHMEN

A primary source of insight comes from biblical theologians who are reassessing the life of the church in the light of the New Testament. Some reflections that are giving a clearer focus to the meaning of churchmanship were set forth by the early apostles. Peter affirmed that the church represented "the people of God." They were the persons who answered the question asked of every man as it was asked of Adam: "Where are you" (in relation to me)? They are the ones who seek to be related to God in faith and trust, and hope. These are the people who, like the Hebrews that gathered at Shechem with Joshua, acknowledged with thanksgiving their deliverance from slavery into freedom. They could have gathered in the temple at Jerusalem, or the synagogues in Babylonia during the dispersion, or the Upper Room at Jerusalem after the resurrection of Jesus, to acknowledge their dependence upon God in all of life's relationships and their moral obligation to live by his imperatives. (See I Peter 2:9.)

Luke declares that the church is the fellowship of the spirit. (Acts 2:42.) It comes about through personal relationship to Christ rather than the relationship between man and man. It is a community of those persons whose spirit has been transformed by the spirit of Christ, who have been quickened by his spirit. They are guided by the spirit of Christ in all of life's relationships. Churchmanship involves participation in the life of the fellowship under the influence of the spirit of Christ.

Paul asserts that the church is "one body in Christ" (Rom. 12:5). It represents the corpus, the living embodiment, of the spirit of Christ. The members of this body need to keep in continuous relationship with the head, seeking the mind of Christ, being guided in their decisions by his influence. Christ is the source of wholeness, healing, and health in their lives.

All these metaphors refer to the church that is gathered. There are other images in the New Testament that refer to the church dispersed. Luke points to the church scattered as "the followers of the way." (Acts 19:23 ff.) They were the persons who challeged the silversmiths in the market place when they declared they believed in one God and that the purchase of the whole pantheon of God's built by the artisans was a concession to idolatry. They called upon people to give their ultimate loyalty to Yahweh, the one God of heaven and earth. This was the church at witness in the world.

Likewise the early church set forth to be of service in the world. The ministry of Jesus and that of his followers were one continuing ministry. The early church was summoned to equip "the saints, for the work of ministry" (Eph. 4:12). The forms which this service has taken as well as the structures through which it has operated have changed from age to age. Yet the ministry that persists is Christ's ministry of reconciliation through which service continues to reconcile the world to God. It is to this response of service as the church in the world that the laity are called and summoned to deport themselves in their daily lives as worthy of this calling. (Eph. 4:1-3.)

Parallel with the ministry of witness and service in the early New Testament church went the function of mission. Interestingly, Luke usually refers to apostles in mission as persons sent by a group. Peter and John are sent to Samaria (Acts 8:14), Paul and Barnabas are sent forth from Antioch (Acts 13:1-4) by the church. These men with a mission work as teams (Acts 13); yet it is clear that differences of function begin to emerge. Paul, Barnabas, Timothy, Titus, all preach the word and perform pastoral functions, but the apostle Paul seems to develop a system of control over other ministries. (II Tim. 4:12.) It is also clear that the persons sent as missionaries had a variety of gifts and competencies. They had target audiences to which they were sent. Above all, they were called to be stewards responsible to the body which sent them. Mission in the early church never meant individuals going on their own; it was planned by the Christian community as part of the wider ministry.

With vivid frequency we find names like people, body, fellowship, followers, servants, sent people who risk being guided by the influence of God upon their lives. These people are the church in biblical perspective. The church, then, is not a club that human beings join on their own terms. Nor is it an exhibition hall for moral do-gooders. Rather, it is a community of believers who acknowledge their relationship established by God, who accept it and respond to it in faith and love. The heightened awareness of this relationship is the source of their worship and the continuing incentive for study to know the mind of Christ. It is the inner compulsion for service in the world, the power behind their work. As churchmen they find meaning and fulfillment for their lives as they gather for worship, study, and fellowship, and scatter for witness, service, and mission work.

The revival of interest in and understanding of the biblical images of the church enable laymen to gain a new perspective on the meaning of churchmanship.

NEW INSIGHTS OF LAYMEN

A further source causing the church to reassess its way of operating today comes from the experiences of laymen in their work and community activities.

Many time-honored concepts are being reevaluated in community life. Kenneth Herrold reports on a careful experiment of leadership in government: "Leadership is exhibited by different people at different times, depending on the task to be done and upon the composition of the group." [2] In a study of the domineering type of a business executive, Chris Argyris indicates that employees have fairly high morale because they believe that such a leader will help them to keep their job. The records show that a plant with such an executive has low waste and higher profits. Among the employees, however, there is tension, conflict, apple-polishing in a scramble for higher position. "Directive leadership may pay off in dollar profits, but it does not develop leadership for tomorrow from the followers of today." [3]

---

[2] *Leadership in Action*, Selected Reading Series TWO, National Training Laboratories, NEA. Article, "The Scientific Spotlight on Leadership," by Kenneth Herrold, p. 4.

[3] *Ibid.*, "Research Trends in Executive Behavior," Chris Argyris, p. 13.

In conferences of churchmen the long tradition of designated leadership in the church is being reviewed in the light of these new concepts and given serious reconsideration. The rise of the lay movement takes an effective part in the life of the decision-making and planning councils of the church. There is an increasing awareness among churchmen that what happens to the creative powers in the development of persons is important for evaluating churchmanship. The conditions of rapid cultural change make the continuous reeducation of people by the more insightful and competent ones imperative. "Our sociological theories, our political philosophy, our practical maxims of business, our political economy, and our doctrines of education are derived from an unbroken tradition and practical examples from the age of Plato," says A. N. Whitehead, former professor of philosophy at Harvard. "The whole of this tradition is warped by the vicious assumption that each generation will substantially live amid the conditions governing the lives of their fathers and will transmit these conditions to mold with equal force the lives of its children. We are living in the first period of human history for which this assumption is false." [4]

Toward Experiment and Exploration

If these changing cultural forces are moving at such a rate that the experience of a former generation is obsolete as a guide for our understanding of the universe in the space age and our conduct of human relations in the age of instant communication, then we may need to reassess the decision-making and administrative processes in the church. We may need to redistribute authority and to search for new solutions in a climate of mutual trust. We may need to move from the security of traditional procedures into a period of inquiry, invention, and testing of new ways of functioning and relating to one another

[4] *Adventure of Ideas*, p. 117.

in the Christian community. In actuality, a church moves toward its goals to the extent that people understand and support its life and mission and accept responsibility for embodying the spirit of Christ in the world rather than being controlled by the passing cultural pressures of the community.

THE EMERGENCE OF MUTUAL MINISTRY

In short, as lay persons reassess the potentialities and liabilities of churchmanship on the present scene, they are discovering that it is necessary now for the church to move toward mutual ministry between churchmen.

Basically, mutual ministry is an interactional phenomenon. It describes the cooperative relationship between clergy and laity, persons in the church who have a concern for one another. It recognizes that persons who may be designated to do certain jobs are recipients of influences from other persons throughout the church, that they both give and take within the church. Mutual ministry looks upon the entire Christian community of clergy and laity alike as persons under the guidance of the Holy Spirit seeking to discover the will of God for their lives. Clergy and laity seek to help each other to understand the work which Christ would have the church undertake in his name today. The goals they seek are shared goals, chosen in keeping with the message and mission of the church.

REASSESS CLERGY-LAITY ROLES

If the laity, as Hendrik Kraemer suggests, are to become "unfrozen" for this work of mutual ministry, the church must clarify the roles of clergy and laity so that they embody the biblical perspective, the tradition of the church, and are relevant to the present needs of the world. If it expects laymen to participate in the tasks of embodying the Christian faith in life's relationships, it must clarify these expectations, rebuild its educational system to support them, and train adults in the affirmations of churchmenship that give visible reality to the faith which it professes. In *The Church and Its Laity,* Georgia Harkness declares that the early church assumed that all people were called by God to acknowledge their relationship to him, to share in God's gift of redemption, and to support the church in accordance with their talents.[5] The church was not an entity people joined, rather, they publicly acknowledged their relationship to God and expressed it daily in their lives. Today life is regarded in a much less religious way. It is urbane, secular, technological. Does the concept of the "priesthood of believers" still have relevance for a secular world? Howard Grimes contends that it is the obligation of the laity to witness to their faith in relevant ways in such a world.[6] Moreover, it is the educational task of the church to prepare the adults for this witness in the world. Impossible, says Peter Berger who claims that the churches of today are passive supporters of the "status quo" of society and that their people are thus incapable of rising above the routines of life to new vision or critique.[7] Therefore the churches merely confuse men and women causing them to identify themselves with the particular bias of their culture and to believe that it is the ultimate value of the Christian religion.

If the churches, because of cultural captivity, retreat from the task of preparing adults for ministries in the world, a new kind of clericism will arise that is wholly inept in this secular world. This is the assertion of Gibson Winter.[8] The more the clergy are called upon to deal with alcoholics, settle labor disputes, reconcile the divorced, give street demonstrations of brotherhood, the more are they preempting the ministry of the laity in the world.

This reversal of roles creates an anomaly in the churches. More

[5] *The Church and Its Laity,* pp. 26-27.
[6] *The Rebirth of the Laity,* p. 105.
[7] *The Noise of Solemn Assemblies,* pp. 101-4.
[8] *The New Creation as Metropolis,* pp. 46-47.

and more laymen are now occupying pulpits for the preachers, while ministers move out into the secular world to give visible witness to the impact of the gospel in contemporary life. If the laity move to confine Christianity to inner piety within the walls of newly constructed sanctuaries, we are on the verge of a new kind of lay monasticism in urban life. This practice denies that God is the Lord of all history. Until the clergy can reassess their roles in the light of the New Testament injunction "for the equipment of the saints, for the work of ministry," [9] and work with the laity to develop inner spiritual understanding as well as freedom and competence to become communicators of the Christian faith in the world, the church cannot fulfill its mission in the midst of the population explosion and the knowledge and technological revolution of our time.

Chapter 1
Bibliography

Adorno, T. W. *The Authoritarian Personality*. New York: Harper Bros., 1950.

Baird, W. *The Corinthian Church*. Nashville: Abingdon Press, 1964.

Berger, Peter. *The Noise of Solemn Assemblies*. Garden City, N. Y.: Doubleday, 1961.

Berton, P. *The Comfortable Pew*. Philadelphia: Lippincott, 1965.

Grimes, Howard. *The Rebirth of the Laity*. Nashville: Abingdon Press, 1962.

Harkness, Georgia. *The Church and Its Laity*. Nashville: Abingdon Press, 1962.

Howe, Reuel. *Herein Is Love*. Valley Forge, Pa.: Judson Press, 1961.

[9] *Eph.* 4:12.

Hunter, Floyd. *Top Leadership, U.S.A.* Chapel Hill, N. C.: University of N. C. Press, 1959.

Leadership in Action (N.T.L.–N.E.A.) Washington, D. C.

Rokeach, Milton. *The Open and Closed Mind.* New York: Basic Books, 1960.

Whitehead, A. N. *Adventure of Ideas.* New York: Macmillan, 1933.

Winter, G. *The New Creation as Metropolis.* New York: Macmillan, 1963.

Chapter 2

The Lay Potential in Perspective

How did the church arrive at its present situation? Does the perspective of church history throw any light upon our paths? Are the emerging images of churchmanship realizable? Are laymen so fixed in old routines that they cannot change? These questions demand an answer from any church leader who faces the transition of the present age in search of solutions to the new demands upon the church.

PERSPECTIVE DETERMINES RELATIONSHIPS

The way a church leader looks at the laity will determine in large measure the way he relates to them. If one views the laity as a collection of advice-giving moralists who use their value systems as a weapon to bring others into conformity, then one's

shield of defense goes up immediately. If one views the laity as
sensitive persons who seek to understand the anxieties and hostilities of other people, then churchmen will relate to them
as fellow sinners in search of God's love and will. If adults are
perceived as a power block that is seeking to use the program
of the church for their own ends, a leader will proceed to enlarge their knowledge of the life and mission of the church. If
adults are perceived as persons who are seeking to participate
in the life of Christian faith, then the leader will continue
to expand the areas of responsibility for service and to provide
the kinds of support that enable them to be the church. If a person perceives adults as arrested in their development, seeking
to know the Bible only as a storybook, then he will proceed
to move from superficiality to some understandings of the great
essential unity and message of the Gospels. If a church leader
perceives them as mature minds who are inquiring more deeply
into the Christian way of life, he will proceed in ways that help
them discover meanings which they may appropriate personally
and communicate in their relationships with others. One's perspective determines in a very large way his attitudes and procedures toward the laity of the church. There is a large variety
of laymen in the church. They represent many levels of maturity
and development. Hence flexibility and adaptibility in relating to
them is paramount.

CONTEMPORARY IMAGES OF MAN

The church exists in a society that has many well-defined
ways of looking at its contemporaries. The vast amusement industry looks upon men and women as pleasure-seeking animals
who will pay millions each year to satisfy these cravings. The
educator looks upon contemporary men and women as minds
with an insatiable hunger for knowledge and skills, with un-
developed potentials for lifelong learning, and an unfulfilled desire for the good life. The merchant and the economist look

upon their fellowmen as consumers with inexhaustible needs for possessing gadgets, gimmicks, and the material things of life. The scientist looks upon mankind as master over the forces of the universe through the use of methods by which to present hypotheses and experiments, and verify his conclusions. Many politicians look upon man as an individual who believes that he can attain the good way of life through the use of governmental power for social purposes.

THREE FACTORS IN A NEW APPROACH

In the midst of these conflicting views of man, the church must interpret its perception of laymen clearly and responsibly. This means going beyond credal formulations and stating this view in terms by which it seeks to enable men and women to live in the church and in society. In formulating its view the church must reassess what has happened to the lives of men and women in America in recent years, review its historical relationship with the laity, and bring intelligent theological perspective to bear upon its formula. It must bring these perspectives together in a new creative synthesis and resolve to live with its new understanding.

SOME BASIC FACTS ABOUT MODERN MAN

During the past century the life span has been extended by at least twenty years. People are healthier and therefore capable of more activity. Simultaneously the work week has decreased from seventy hours a week in 1850 to fifty-five hours a week in 1900 to forty in 1950, and has now moved down to thirty-five to forty hours per week. With increased time each week and good means of travel, we confront increased mobility. The nation-wide system of excellent highways gives access to all parts of the country. Moreover, early retirement from work is becoming much more widespread. Older adults have many more leisure years on their hands. Increasingly each adult has many more units of energy at his command to use as he determines. In 1900, persons had about 1030 horsepower hours to use each year. In 1950, this had moved to 4470. If one projects the amounts of energy to be used in the future, the results are fantastic. At the same time, machines have taken over more of the work in the world. One hundred years ago human beings and animals were doing the larger share of the work of the world; today machines produce ninety-eight per cent of the goods and services for mankind.[1] Between 1890 and 1900 the average adult completed between six and eight years of schooling. Today the median is high-school graduation and is moving toward the first year of college. Likewise the average income per person has risen from $ 833 per person in 1900 to more than $ 2000 per person in the 1960's. When viewed together, these factors would indicate that laymen today live longer, are healthier, better educated, have more time, and the power to command tremendous sources of energy to do their bidding. These factors need to be assessed correctly as the church views the potential of the laity. In his provocative study, *Of Time, Work, and Leisure,* Sebastian De Grazia asserts, "The wisdom of the world was madness if, in teaching men how to subdue nature and transform the earth, it made them turn their back on life." [2] Basically, here are indices of the potential for the laity to be the church. These factors must not be obscured by subjective feelings. They are clues to the laity toward the work of real ministry.

SOME HISTORICAL FACTORS THAT INFLUENCE THE PRESENT

Any real assessment of the lay potential in the church needs to bring into clear focus the long history of lay relationship in the church. In any crisis it is likely to come up for reassessment. Any new design in church organization and function needs to review

[1] Cf. C. Tibbitts and Wilma Donahue, *Aging in the Modern World,* pp. 27-28.

[2] P. 3.

and reappraise former structures, the contributions which laymen have made, and the problems which the church has encountered. We are a people of God with a history. We can learn from that history.

In the early church people had a sense of their calling (Eph. 4:11-16), and when the selection of officials became necessary, laymen participated in the choosing of deacons (Acts 6). Paul instructed laymen to come together in fellowship and sing, teach, and interpret the Scriptures (I Cor. 14:26). Clement at Rome invited them to participate in the Eucharist by bringing bread, wine, and offerings. Tertullian urged them to meet in homes for a love feast. "After washing of hands and lighting of lamps, individual members are invited to stand out and to sing to the best of their ability from sacred scriptures. . . . The feast ends with prayer" (Apology, 39).[3] So it was that the laity who provided the ingredients of the sacraments and engaged in acts of worship to God. In its inception worship involved the laity in working out their right relationship to God. It was not a performance. The laity were participants in the act of worship, not spectators who observed someone else at worship.

ROLE OF DISCIPLESHIP IN THE EARLY CHURCH

The role of the layman as a parent was quite clear in the early church. It was his Christian duty to share his faith and provide discipline in morals for his children. This duty could not be delegated. (Col. 3:21.) It was the advice of St. John Chrysostom that fathers should train their sons; mothers their daughters. They were to teach religious history beginning with the stories of the heroes of the Old Testament. They were urged to tell two stories at a time: Cain and Abel, Jacob and Esau. Three weeks later, advised Chrysostom, say to the child, "Tell me the stories of the two brothers." When he starts, say, "No, I

[3] Stephen C. Neill and Hans-Ruedi Weber, *The Layman in Christian History*, p. 35.

don't mean that one. I mean the other one." Early in life they
began to distinguish between Christian life and faith and the
world about them.[4] Even children were to perceive that life had
alternatives and that they were to make decisions about them.
The stories were not told for entertainment purposes. They were
not ends in themselves. They were means whereby parents could
help their children to think about life from a biblical perspective
and clarify alternatives.

Before anyone could be baptized in the early church, he was
instructed in the catechism. By A.D. 180 laymen in Rome were
placed on probation for three years of study in a carefully graded
course. In the beginning laymen were instructors; later this task
was taken over by priests and bishops. The practice spread and
Gregory of Nyssa, Cyril in Jerusalem, and Theodore of
Mopsuestia developed excellent catechetical studies. These studies for churchmen did not end with baptism; they went on
throughout life, becoming deeper and more comprehensive.
Growth and maturity were expected to result from the study
of the Christian faith.

The challenge of Gnosticism rejecting the Jewish Scriptures,
the attack of Celsus against Origen, the heresy of Marcion, the
pressure of Roman culture and its mystery religions caused the
bishops of the early church to meet in councils and formulate
the creeds of the church. The attacks from the Roman state
which brought martyrdom to churchmen developed the ethic
of "being in the world but not of the world." Christians were
guided to take part as citizens but not to endorse Roman
morality. They were to abandon the circus, stay away from public
baths, and shun sexual promiscuity. They were to trust God,
show kindness, and witness in persecution. Eusebius, in his description of events preceding the martyrdom of Polycarp, relates
an incident about Germanicus, "who, strengthened by divine

---

[4] H. I. Marrou, *A History of Education in Antiquity*, p. 420.

grace, overcame the natural dread of death implanted in us, spurned the entreaties of the proconsul. He, however, hesitated not, but eagerly irritated the wild beast against him, . . . that he might the sooner be freed from the unjust and lawless generation." [5] Under the impact of these two forces, namely: (a) persecution by the state, and (b) heresy from within, the clerical leadership of the church forged basic formulas of the faith and became defenders of it against these attacks.

Although the early church fathers resisted the culture of the Roman Empire, they accepted the established schools and the Greek heritage which they imparted. They knew that an education was needed to participate in the liturgy, to interpret the Scripture to the children, and for mission. They accepted the Greco-Roman view of man as able to perform acts of faith and morally worthy deeds. They listened to the great questions about life formulated by Greek thinkers and urged the individual to open himself to the grace of God offered a Christian, receive the sacrament of baptism, and avow that Jesus was Lord. In doing so, a layman had to realize the limits of the culture that had nurtured him and relate his life to a more ultimate reality.

GROWING POWER OF THE CLERGY IN THE CHURCH

Although the Christian fathers continued a stream of criticism against pagan gods and customs, they did not set up a parochial school system, nor ask to take their pupils out of Roman schools. The antidote was provided by the parents through religious training in the home. In fact, many Christian laymen became teachers in classical schools. Origen, in A.D. 202-3, accepted such a job to support his family after the martyrdom of his father. Even the efforts of Emperor Julian, in A.D. 362, to forbid Christians to teach were short-lived. His attempts to paganize the schools completely brought on some rather ingenious reactions

[5] *Ecclesiastical History,* Book IV, chap. XV.

by Christian parents and scholars. They rewrote the Pentateuch in Homeric Greek style, other Old Testament books as odes, dramas, etc. The New Testament was rewritten in the style of the dialogues of Plato. Thus, by learning the biblical treasures written in these classical styles, both the biblical faith and Greco-Roman heritage were preserved. In A.D. 364 the ban of Julian was lifted, Christian teachers went back to school, and the pupils returned to the classical tradition without much difficulty.[6]

Under periods of duress or enlightenment, adult laymen of the early church provided a vital link between the church and the world. Through worship and discipleship, witnessing and serving, they found ways of showing forth a "life worthy of their calling." Although they had less and less influence in the inner councils of the church, by the time of Constantine they were recognized as factors in the world which matched the ecclesiastical domination within the church structure. During the first four centuries the early church moved from "ecclesia" as an assembly of the whole people of God to an ecclesiastical system as a policy-making and functioning organization in which the clergy were dominant sources of authority.

THE FREEZING OF CLERGY-LAITY RELATIONSHIPS IN THE MIDDLE AGES

After the fall of the Roman Empire, the church and society began to rebuild their relationships on a new set of assumptions. Augustine had set them down in *The City of God* which portrayed two realms: (a) the city of earth in which man is ruled by pride and self-love; (b) the city of God created out of divine love. The "civitas terrana" was the secular realm in which the emperor became ruler and warrior, and serfs became the inhabitants. The "civitas dei" was the domain of pope, bishop, priest, and monk who were designated to keep faith and learning

[6] H. I. Marrou, *A History of Education in Antiquity*, p. 342.

alive. As monastic orders grew, the church leaders were housed in monasteries wherein they were cut off from the world. Schools were set up primarily for the clergy. The role of the clergy and laity became fixed. If you were born a serf you remained a serf. All classes and functions in society were frozen. The kings and noblemen built palaces around which the serfs tilled the soil, sharing the fruit of the lands with the lord for the protection of castles when the lands were invaded. Between these two realms there was a chasm of difference and a continuous struggle for power. It came to its climax when Charlemagne was crowned Emperor of the Holy Roman Empire on Christmas Day A.D. 800 and made defender of the churches against pagans.

With the rise of lay rulers who presided over affairs of church and state came the division of lands into parishes and the assessment of a compulsory tithe upon all landlords for the support of the church. (See Lev. 27:30.) During this period a great advance in the building of parish churches took place. The ascent of Gregory VII in the eleventh century brought the rise of the papacy over both church and state with absolute authority.

The religious life of the layman consisted of reciting each day the Lord's prayer and the creed, and attending matins and mass on Sunday. He was the recipient of the sacrament from the clergy who began strengthening the hold these ecclesiastical rites had upon an illiterate constituency through a system of discipline including confession, penance, and absolution. Laymen were defenders of the faith. This role they fulfilled tragically through the crusades in which laymen who wished to express their zeal were misled. The church was unable to guide them, and most of the results were disastrous for all.

THE RENAISSANCE SPURRED CLERGY AND LAITY TO NEW ACTIVITY

The rise of Bible-reading in the twelfth century gave new impetus to religious thought and discussion. It was the reading of the words of the gospel that brought the awakening to Francis of Assisi who founded the brotherhood which ministered to the poor. These works of charity in an order predominantly of lay friars represented one of the first attempts in centuries of the church to move out of the monastic halls to serve the world.

Monasticism—the life of a search for salvation through solitariness—characterized the monks in the monasteries. "Poverty, chastity, and obedience," the Benedictine rule, was the guide for the monastic life of prayers, withdrawal, and meditation. It was a life that responded to "vocation"—a calling by God. Later the Benedictines established an order of "secular clergy" who were to serve in the world by feeding the hungry and by dignified manual labor in the field. The activity which stands above all else was contemplation of God by the "religious."

The educational life of the people languished from the fall of Rome until the twelfth century. Episcopal schools were set up in the cathedrals of some bishops for the training of clergy. Some monasteries gathered boys for teaching, but general education was not extant. In the thirteenth century the Dominicans, a learned order of priests, set about to reform the educational training of the clerics. When the universities began to spring up later, these priests staffed the college halls. It was under a Dominican, Albert Magnus, that Thomas Aquinas studied at the University of Paris. He later developed a new synthesis between man's relation to the truth of God and knowledge of the world which has become a monumental formulation of the Christian faith for all time.

CHANGING ROLES OF LAYMEN IN THE REFORMATION

The vast changes that brought about the rise of Protestant movements, the emergence of national states in Europe and a new economic system, plunged laymen into many new roles. Sir Thomas More, Philip of Hesse, Zwingli in Zürich, and Caspar Schwenckfeld exercised great influence in the changing laws and political structures that reflected the emerging moral values. Tyndale and Wycliff became instrumental in the translation of the Bible into the language of the people. Dürer, Cranach, Grünewald were the creators of new art forms, and later Bach and Händel gave musical expression to the spiritual breakthrough. Laymen became instrumental in formulating the culture and spirit of the new age.

Crucial in fostering these changes was the shift in theological perspective expounded by Martin Luther. In affirming the "priesthood of all believers," the German reformer asserted all persons have the same basic relationship to God. Each has direct access to God without need of a mediator. Faith was the primary requisite. There are no persons with special status. Each person also is his own priest who must make sacrifice for his neighbor. This doctrine was a basic challenge to the clergy-laity relationships that permeated the Middle Ages. Not only did it give credence to the Reformation, it provides a base for rethinking clergy-laity relationships today.

A second great affirmation of Luther which changed the perspective of the laity was "justification by faith." As he put it,

I stood before God as a sinner troubled in conscience, and I had no confidence that my merit would assuage him. Therefore I did not love a just and angry God, but rather hated and murmured against him. . . . Night and day I pondered until I saw the connection between the justice of God and the statement that "the just shall live by his faith." Then I grasped that the justice of God is that righteousness by which through grace and sheer mercy God justifies us through faith.[7]

This affirmation lit a torch of new freedom. In actual practice, however, the pastor in the German churches retained much of

[7] Roland H. Bainton, *Here I Stand*, p. 65.

the same power and authority that the priest held during the Middle Ages.

The Reformation broke up the former relations of church and state. The rise of the national states in which laymen, schooled in the law, gained new eminence, broke sharply with the absolute power of church over state. In Germany the princes chose the type of religion for their own domain. In England the crown insisted on being head of church and state. In Zürich laymen combined religion and patriotism so that councils regulated morals, preaching, and church attendance. In Sweden Gustavus Adolphus chose and defended the Lutheran faith. In Geneva John Calvin kept control of city and church through a system of elders who were laymen in control of church councils and who kept the morals of the city enforced. Elders and deacons of the church were nominated and approved by councils. Through these swift events laymen became recognized as the force in the church who brought Christian ethics to worldly practices.

Reform inside the church made the practices of worship more meaningful to the faithful. Laymen were encouraged to study the Bible which was translated and printed in their own languages for greater distribution. Likewise, printed prayerbooks and hymnbooks enabled the people to enter into the liturgies which formerly were said or sung by priests. In the sacrament of the Lord's Supper, the cup formerly drunk by the priest was given to all believers. In this practice "all believers were priests," as Luther affirmed. From these reforms the way was opened again for meaningful participation in worship by the laity.

SECTARIANISM FRAGMENTS THE CHURCH

The reaction to absolute authority which began in the Reformation continued as the Protestant movement became entrenched in Northern Europe. New movements gathered around emerging personalities giving rise to sectarianism. The Anabaptists broke with the Lutheran leaders by insisting upon the "authority of the Inner Word" over against Luther's insistence upon the revelation of the *Word*. The Schwenckfelders contended for a radical individualism based on the Spirit. In contrast, the Hutterite Brethren formed a producing and consuming economy to preserve their colony "until Christ should come again." The followers of Menno Simons insisted on separation of church and state and refused to bear arms when the government sought to wage war. These sects placed new emphasis on voluntary association of believers, decreased the significance of the sacraments, and set up new tensions between church and world. The new freedom which began as reform of the church fragmented "the body of Christ" into numerous sects divided by differing emphases of doctrine and led by colorful personalities.[8] This was the first time in the long history of the church that such splintering had taken place.

Both state church and sectarian movement found fertile soil along the American frontiers for colonizing and transplanting their particular belief systems. Anglican establishments grew in Virginia and New York. The Puritans controlled Massachusetts. The Quakers colonized Pennsylvania, while Lord Baltimore claimed Maryland for the Catholics. In the climate of tolerance that pervaded the peaceful colony of William Penn, the Mennonites, the Dunkers, the followers of Schwenckfeld, and the Moravian Brethren found a new haven.

In a new land with expanding frontiers, lay preachers and cults of religious minorities built around lay leaders thrived. They produced a situation in which no major religious group prevailed and each survived by tolerance of the others. Moreover, Rhode Island under Roger Williams became the first place where church and state were completely separate. This principle established a new freedom and placed religion, in one place in the United

[8] Cf. F. Littell, *The Origins of Sectarian Protestantism*, pp. 21-43.

States, upon a basis of voluntarism. In such a situation leadership arose from the free associations of the people. Lay preachers, circuit riders, exhorters, class leaders served this mobile people. Revivals, camp meetings, evangelical campaigns, prayer meetings characterized both the dynamic and unstructured ways of religious life. Later the Sunday school movement recruited thousands of lay volunteers for teaching, while men's work and women's work evolved as forces giving impetus to the missionary, evangelical, and stewardship work of churches as their organizations became more stable and more structured.

THE LAITY POTENTIAL IN REVIEW

Viewed in perspective, the potentialities of the laity today are enormous. Contemporary laity are the healthiest in the history of mankind, the best educated, and destined for greater participation in the life of the Christian community.

There are leaders who claim that the laymen are so tradition-bound that they cannot change. This review of the laymen in church history refutes the notion that laymen are fixed in old routines. The perspective of history reflects many changing roles for laymen. When the church was persecuted by the state, laymen kept Christian faith alive in their homes. When civilization was destroyed, they preserved the faith in their own souls through piety, prayer, and practices of worship. After the Reformation the laymen were the creators of a new culture. They wrote the laws, the new music, the new literature, and reconstructed the institutions of society. They have survived and found ways of witnessing even under the absolute authority of church and state. They have led and been misled. They have been faithful and faithless. They have fought for freedom and participated in the splitting of the church. Throughout all these situations they have exhibited a tremendous potential for giving expression to the Christian faith as they understood it.

WHERE THEN DOES THE PROBLEM LIE?

The problem calls for a much clearer statement by church leaders concerning the role of the laity. Do church leaders want the laity to be institutional maintenance men who help the preacher "run the church"? Do church leaders want the laity to be spectators while the minister says their prayers and the choir sings their affirmation of faith? Do church leaders really want laymen to be the church in the world? What kind of support, responsible guidance, and mutual ministry will the church provide for the layman who tries it?

From this cursory survey of the lay potential in the church it has become clear that, when the church leaders have defined the roles of the laity clearly, laymen have tended to fulfill them adequately. When confusion was created by forces outside the church or inside the Christian community or through silence of leadership, the laity, and eventually the clergy, have become inept, apathetic, and disenchanted. If unity of purpose, mutual ministry, renewal in the church, reunion among the fragments of the Body of Christ, and the emergence of a new life together in the church are to become a part of God's action in the church in our time, church leaders must clarify what they believe God expects of clergy and laity in the space age.

Chapter 2
Bibliography

Augustine, Saint. *The City of God.* Modern Library. 1950.
Bainton, Roland H. *Here I Stand.* Nashville: Abingdon Press, 1951.
De Grazia, Sebastian. *Of Time, Work, and Leisure.* New York: Twentieth Century, 1962.

Eusebius. *Ecclesiastical History*. London: George Bell & Sons, 1897.

Gustafson, James M. *Treasure in Earthen Vessels: The Church as a Human Community*. New York: Harper & Bros., 1961.

Harkness, Georgia. *John Calvin*. Nashville: Abingdon Press, 1958.

Leete, Frederick DeLand. *Christian Brotherhoods*. Cincinnati: Jennings & Graham, 1912.

Littell, Franklin H. *The Origins of Sectarian Protestantism*. New York: Macmillan, 1964.

Manschreck, Clyde. *Melanchthon: The Quiet Reformer*. Nashville: Abingdon Press, 1958.

Marrou, Henri I. *A History of Education in Antiquity*. London: Sheed, 1956.

Also: A Mentor Book, The New American Library, 1964.

Neill, Stephen C. and Weber, Hans-Ruedi (eds.). *The Layman in Christian History*. Philadelphia: Westminster Press, 1963.

Religion in Life, Winter, 1961.

Tibbitts, C. and Donahue, Wilma. *Aging in the Modern World*. Ann Arbor: University of Michigan Press, 1957.

Chapter 3

What May Churches Expect of Laymen Today?

The preacher was irate. "Why did Mrs. Wells not show up tonight? She knows," he continued, "that the women need her to serve that spaghetti supper." As we strolled toward the dining room, I tried to reduce his feeling of tension by commenting, "Maybe something happened at home to detain her." Incensed by this inadvertent remark, he turned and retorted, "No! She's down at that School Board meeting."

Confused Expectations Concerning Laymen

Immediately a series of images, questions, and impressions began to well up within my mind. What was this preacher's image of the church, the church gathered, the church scattered? What did he think of the role of the laity? Was a spaghetti supper in

44

the church more important than being a living witness to the meaning of the Christian spirit in the decision-making institutions of the community? What does it mean to be the church in the world?

Three weeks later I found myself at a church dinner in another city. Seated across from me was the mayor whose anxieties were plainly showing. As I listened, his consternation began to unravel. "Today I presented the hospital budget. They cut $50,000 off the cancer research appropriation. As I looked around, four of my Christian friends were missing," he continued with a staccato pace. "I suppose they were all out there chasing the almighty dollar. And I thought Christians were supposed to support the health of people in the community."

Small wonder that laymen are confused. Is their role that of spectator, viewing the performance of the Sunday worship service and serving an occasional church dinner? Are they called to "be the church" in their homes, on their jobs, during their leisure, and in the community?

A NEW SELF-IMAGE IS NEEDED

After these two experiences, I began to inquire into the laymen's impressions. "What does the idea of being the church mean to you?" I asked. The replies were varied and not too insightful. They included: more committee meetings; knocking on doors; larger contributions to the budget; being the minister's helper; busy work to keep the institution going; doing the ushering. One came up with: to preach sermons like the preacher. These replies led me to the conclusion that clergymen have looked too long upon the laymen as "the taught, the preached to, and the led." Continuous practice that imbeds these images into the consciousness of the laity lulls them into apathy. Character research has found that the level of expectancy determines the behavior of persons more than any other single factor. If laymen are to be churchmen today, they must obtain a new self-image and understanding of the meaning of the church, and retrain for responsible participation in the life of the Christian community. If laymen are to overcome their spectatoritis in worship, their overdependence on power figures in decision-making, and the tendency to salvation through status-seeking, they must get a new assessment of themselves as churchmen and a new description of their functions.

Adults who come to the church today seek courage and meaning for their lives. The churches try to communicate the gospel to them in ways that make sense. The danger lies in a perversion of the gospel on the one hand and in noncommunication on the other. The church seeks to relate the persistent lifelong concerns of men to a reality that is beyond taste, touch, smell, and the other confining aspects of physical environment. Innumerable adults seek answers to these same concerns by running away into sensationalism, erratic religion, or despair. In so doing, they miss the mark of being human. Some persons in our culture revert to adolescent irresponsibility by becoming inefficient cogs in a company machine or turn and become hostile destroyers of our social institutions. They miss the mark of becoming authentic persons. Plagued by hidden fear, many persons try to find security by buying more and more material goods. They refuse to acknowledge their involvement, the perplexities of suffering and death. All these persons need a new vision of who they are and what they can become. For them the church has a message of "good news."

THE GOOD NEWS WHICH THE CHURCH COMMUNICATES

The good news which the church offers can come as a saving reality to these men and women. It tells human beings that God endows them with capacities for responsible participation in life. It claims that man is never so completely trapped by the circumstances of life that he cannot approach God who transcends these circumstances. It claims that through faith in Christ he can rise above their enmeshing coils and assess life from a higher perspective. The good news is that men were not born for estrangement and alienation. It contends that God accepts man, loves him, and is creatively and redemptively at work to bring him into right relationship with reality and his fellowmen. This is the "good news" of man's true destiny. When this relationship is restored, man can accept both life and death with a sense of dependency upon God. Through worship, fellowship, and study the church communicates to man a new sense of identity that can redeem him from pretense and from running away into the lures of nonauthentic existence. It enables him to find courage and personal meaning for his life.

PARTICIPATION IN THE LIFE OF FAITH

The church is not satisfied to enable persons to gain a new self-image; it summons men to new understandings of the saving work which Christ has done for mankind. The faith which the church interprets is not merely rational acceptance of a set of propositions. It is more. The faith which the church inspires is trust that involves risk. The faith which the church inculcates in adults involves the reorientation of their whole beings. It is a total response of the self to a gift of God who makes man aware of new dimensions and possibilities of life. It is a way of moving into and sharing a whole new realm of freedom that is far beyond man's measurements of life. It is participation in a new way of existing that can transcend old barriers and inner pre-judgments, enabling adults to live with new horizons and a new hope.

Such a faith is made possible through Jesus Christ who revealed to man the lure and power of sin in which he is caught, God's judgment upon it, his mercy toward man who repents and changes, and the reality of a whole new, spiritual realm of time and space. When Jesus heard Peter acknowledge, "You are the Christ," he declared this confession to be the foundation of the church. The church is built of the new beings who find true identity "in Christ." It is the Christian community which came into existence at Pentecost and united all those related to God through Christ into a spiritual fellowship of faith and love which expressed itself in service to those in need. Continued participation in the community of faith through the ages requires understanding of what God has done for man, intelligent response to worship, a life of shared fellowship, witness to one's faith in the world, service to those in need, and devotion to the mission of reconciliation. These roles take on new emphases in the light of today's pressures and the lay potential.

THE RESPONSE OF WORSHIP

The primary response of laymen to the gospel is gratitude. This response is made in the orderly and obedient service of worship. It acknowledges publicly that man is dependent upon God and that God gives meaning and purpose to his life. It involves acts of remembrance, celebration, and rededication. These acts are rooted in the Bible, Christian tradition, teaching, and present participation in the church. The Scriptures, the living tradition of the church, and the guidance by the Holy Spirit make possible the orderly participation of adults in the worship of the church. No adult is ever required to be a spectator who comes to see and hear a preacher perform during worship. While the minister preaches the Word, interprets the Scripture, or leads the congregation in prayer, he guides the people in renewing their relationship with God.

The ways of worship are ordered in the liturgy of the church. Unlike many preconceived notions, worship is not passive enjoyment. It is work! Liturgy is related to the Greek words "laos," people, and "ergon," work, meaning "the work of the people of God." They are seeking their right relation to God—here and now. They are praising God openly for what he has done to redeem them. They are thinking of the ways they can serve

God. They are reformulating in intelligible ways the witness they will make to other persons. They are developing the spiritual resources for the mission of reconciliation.

THE LORD'S SUPPER AS COMMUNICATION

The Lord's Supper is central in the worship of the church. It is the genuine response of the community of Christians to what God has done for them in Christ. It is the gospel reenacted. Through participation the laymen give corporate and visible demonstration that the new "body of Christ" is manifestly alive. (I Cor. 10:16.) The Lord's Supper is an act of remembrance, of communion, and of hope in a future consummation. Through such active words as: "take . . . bless . . . break . . . eat . . . drink," the initiative of God in Christ is remembered in a real and present way. Through meditation, repentance, and prayer the laity recall God's unrelenting judgment upon sin and his faithful forgiveness. Through this action the members of the new community acknowledge the common unity of new persons in Christ which is a foretaste of the unity of mankind in the age to come and of the essential unity of the church with Christ its Lord. The minister is the representative servant of the congregation at the table of the Lord. Through their participation in this sacrament the laymen, as the church visible, proclaim that they have heard the gospel anew and respond in faithfulness and thankfulness.

OBSERVING BAPTISM AS ENTRANCE

Through the sacrament of Baptism persons identify themselves with the dying and rising of Christ. It is the dramatic re-enactment of the washing away of sin and entering into a new life in the Body of Christ. It is a rite of initiation into the Christian community in which the adult "believer" witnesses openly that he has heard "the Word of God," understood it, and is making his response of faith. In churches which practice infant baptism, the whole family acknowledges the prevenient grace of God, and in some cases the whole congregation assumes the role of sponsor for the physical welfare and spiritual nurture of the child until he reaches the age of accountability. Through the influence of committed parents and the responsible nurture by the Christian community, the child is brought to the act of confirmation or conscious decision for membership in the church. The new life in the Christian community into which one enters at baptism involves faithful obedience to the call of God and continuous discipleship in a personal search for meaning of this awakened faith.

Through participation in the observance of worship the laymen proclaim the gospel anew and respond with expectancy and assurance.

DISCIPLESHIP: PARTICIPATION IN LIFELONG LEARNING

Members of the church in every age and culture have found the meaning and expressions of the Christian faith that make it significant and relevant for their lives. They have always been confronted by other faiths and philosophies which denied or attacked the affirmations of the Christian faith. They have always needed to reexamine the grounds of their belief and its implications for the life which they confront. These concerns call for mature participation in learning groups which are more active and creative than listening to instruction and indoctrination. They require adult involvement in honest inquiry, serious testing, and reformulations of beliefs and practices as persons rediscover the meanings of divine activities in a dynamic changing world.

Participation in a community of lifelong learners requires a climate of acceptance and trust in which adults may express their affirmations and doubts. Mature Christians enter into a true dialogue with others. Without pretense they share what they honestly believe, always listen to others, and indicate they have heard their concerns. They lead adults to real confrontation with the Scriptures so that they may discern God revealing himself to man anew. This involves an act of faith. It involves discerning that God who delivered the people from bondage in Egypt was at work in saving mankind through the life, ministry, death, and resurrection of Jesus Christ. It is a matter of faith that the Holy Spirit will lead the studying community into the meaning of these past events as powerful influences upon our lives in the present. This may mean that adult leaders need to translate the language of the Scriptures into a language comprehensible today. They must strive to interpret God's Word with integrity in situations wherein persons are confronted by nonbelievers. Unless there is an honest attempt among adults to hear the Word of God and reshape their lives through understanding it, there is no church. The Body of Christ is found where the living embodiment of the gospel is visible.

The community of adult disciples needs to identify itself with the Christian tradition. No group in the church is composed of isolated individuals who acknowledge no relationship to the basic biblical and historical ways of life. Tradition is the story of interpretation and the mission of the church to every age. It is the corporate life of the church in witness and in teaching from generation to generation. It is the active life of the church in history guided by the Holy Spirit. No group of adult disciples can afford to become so enamored of its own egocentric predicament that it fails to be disciplined by the history of the obedience or disobedience of the church. Tradition lays upon adults the obligation of interpreting to each new generation the good news of God's action in delivering men from evil.

Sharing in experience of discipleship requires sensitivity to the guidance of the Holy Spirit so that adults may discover the meanings of Christian faith for their lives now. This sharing involves more than influencing by example and imitating other persons. It involves more than giving vent to one's moral affirmations while arousing guilt feelings in others. It involves openness, awareness, willingness to change and to adventure in faith. This too is a requirement of participation in the Christian community. By the power of the Spirit the adult participant is enabled to pray, to believe in the continuing presence of Jesus Christ as an influence in his life, and to relate himself to other persons in love and service. Through these relationships teacher and students initiate questions and responses, inquiry and sharing authentically in the encounter of learning. Each calls forth the essential truth which has been revealed in the other through participation in the learning community. Each helps the other discover and clarify the meaning of the Christian faith which he is to embody in his life and share with others in the world. Learning is for witness and discipline in the world.

Growth toward maturity in understanding and participation in the church requires a working knowledge of the Scriptures, tradition, and guidance by the Holy Spirit so that contemporary Christians may be sensitive to the relevant expressions of the Christian way of life today.

FELLOWSHIP: SHARING ONE'S LIFE IN CHRIST

The Christian community calls laymen into fellowship wherein followers and new converts may share their newfound life in Christ. This fellowship is more than conviviality. It is built upon concern for others. Common unity is not togetherness itself; it is a being in Christ, the Head of the church. New understanding becomes reinforced in a fellowship that supports the new way of life.

Likewise Christians in the church today sense a deeper fellowship through their relationship to Christ than they can find in sociability over the coffee cups. In the church they have a new awareness of themselves as spiritual beings. They have a new sensitivity to their freedom and their powers of self-determination. They do not need to relate themselves to one another out of anxiety, because God has offered to forgive them in Christ. Above all, they have the capacity to rise above present conditions and the hope to influence the future. Participation in the fellowship of the church involves being aware of what is happening in the lives of other persons and giving support to their spiritual growth.

LAY APOSTLES: THE CHURCH AT WITNESS

So far, the roles of the laity as worshiper, disciple, and member of a fellowship have been discussed from the perspective of fellowship in the church gathered. But the Christian faith and life can never be contained in four walls. It is embodied in people who go out into the world to witness, to serve, and to be mission. As they discern that God entered the mainstream of life to reconcile the world, they sense that they too are called as the people of God to continue this ministry of reconciliation. This calling is to a shared ministry in their homes, at work, during leisure, and in the structures of society. Apostles are sent people. In the church they are renewed in spirit, informed in mind, and supported in fellowship to go into the world to be the church scattered. As they leave the church building, they enter the church ecumenical—the church involved in the whole fabric of complex structures of society. Herein the layman communicates his faith to the persons and groups that surround him.

The real problem in witnessing to people today is to reach the individual who declares he has no need for God. He does not assert that he is an atheist; he merely affirms that he has the good life now. He has obtained it through the possession of things produced in mass. He is self-sufficient and he knows it. So he has no use for seeking any answers to life's questions in the

Christian tradition. These people are not cloistered in some downtown coffeehouse; they are strolling all about the shopping center. They inhabit the high-rise apartments of our cities in huge numbers. They are the real challenge to the church scattered.

Obviously the church can never confront these persons with the gospel by camouflaging its message in a mess of middle-class values. Here is where Bultmann and Bonhoeffer summon churchmen to rethink what is *message* and what is *myth*. Likewise churchmen are summoned to rethink what is of Christ and what is an accumulation of Western ideas, what is new life in Christ and what is secular personality theory. The call to witness is to new life in Christ—with a new power to be shared and a new meaning for man's existence.

The communication of this message in our time is unmistakably the task of the intelligent Christian layman. He witnesses as he seeks to make the integrity of his relation to God relevant in the world of work. He witnesses as he works through the interpersonal relationships in his family, making it a center of Christian culture. He witnesses as he encounters the encroachments of marketplace morality with a sense of community responsibility. He witnesses to his fellowmen as he discloses a new image of the Christian person.

THE RECOVERY OF SERVANTHOOD

The New Testament calls Christians to serve their fellowmen. With no ulterior motive they are called to give the cup of cold water, or the coat to those in need. Somewhere in the movement of the churches from the inner city to suburbia we have lost the vision of the servanthood of the laity. Perhaps our superhighways and suburban airports have obscured from view the needs of school dropouts, delinquents, trapped slum dwellers, mentally ill persons, the aged and the infirm, or displaced workers whose jobs have been automated. Perhaps the church itself has reduced the role of serving to ushering, putting on suppers, and to chores of institutional maintenance. Servanthood implies much more. It means that the servant has received the grace of God, understood its forgiveness to the extent that he wants to share time, strength, and understanding with others in a helpful way. Because he has a new awareness of who he is, he can relate himself with deeper understanding to other people. Trusting not his own power but the guidance of the Holy Spirit, he can seek to serve others as the living embodiment of discipleship in the contemporary world. Unless churchmen can recover the servanthood role of the laity that enables them to come to grips with the real concerns of the world, the church will move to a place of inconsequential irrelevance in society.

THE SCATTERED CONGREGATION AS MISSION

The Bible affirms that God has acted and continues to act in human history. God delivered the Hebrews from Egyptian bondage, established a moral covenant with his people through Moses, revealed his judgments upon their devious and self-centered undertakings, and reconciled them to a true understanding of themselves and of his relationship to them through Jesus Christ. Awareness of the activity of God is the guiding power in the mission of the church.

It is the task of the congregation to discover where God is at work in the world today, to help persons become aware of it, and to cooperate with his will. As members of a congregation move beyond the doors of the church, they will perceive God's activity differently. Some may see it in the healing acts of hospital, doctors, nurses and share in it as their talents allow. Others may see it as urban renewal and seek to deliver their fellowmen from the scourge of the slums. Others may see God at work in the struggle for more freedom to be human beings and identify themselves with the groups in ways that help them discover

God's will for human life. Others may be called to embody the mission of the church in the communications network so that persons may discover, in image and in idea, what it means to be a human being. Because of their talents, others may be able to bring the deep meanings of the Christian faith to students who are asking relevant questions about life. With wisdom and sensitivity laymen need to observe where God is at work and to respond with faith and obedience.

The church expects the laymen to listen and witness in those situations where people are experiencing the creative and re-demptive processes of God. It expects laymen to make decisions in the light of Christian ethic and to facilitate action which the congregation can support. Laymen are sent into the world to establish justice, unity, and right relations between men and groups. Obviously certain laymen have more talent and skill in some areas of work than in others. These laymen may need guidance in understanding the relevance of the Christian faith for such areas of work, and preparation for dialogue in the world. Through responsible participation in listening to the gospel, re-sponding in worship, studying the implications of the Bible for their living, finding communion in fellowship, they are renewed in mind and spirit for witness, service, and mission in the world.

CONCLUSION

Throughout this chapter one primary implication has pre-vailed. The churches expect laymen to perceive their many roles in the light of biblical Christian faith and not blunt the Chris-tian witness. The churches expect the laymen to participate re-sponsibly in the orders of worship so they may be renewed in spirit, forgiven, and recommitted to service in the world. Churches expect laymen to find that fellowship in depth which enables them to commune with that which is holy, so that they may be sent on mission into the world to establish justice and unity among men.

Chapter 3
Bibliography

Barr, B. *Parish Back Talk*. Nashville: Abingdon Press, 1964.

Come, A. *Agents of Reconciliation*. Philadelphia: Westminster Press, 1959.

Grimes, L. Howard. *The Church Redemptive*. Nashville: Abingdon Press, 1958.

Hardin, H. G., Quillian, J. D., Jr., White, J. F. *The Celebration of the Gospel*. Nashville: Abingdon Press, 1964.

Hunt, George L. and Crow, Paul A., Jr. *Where We Are in Church Union*. New York: Association Press, 1965.

Kirkpatrick, Dow. Oxford Institute on Methodist Theological Studies, *Doctrine of the Church*. Nashville: Abingdon Press, 1962.

Nelson, J. Robert. *Criterion for the Church*. Nashville: Abingdon Press, 1963.

Niebuhr, H. Richard. *The Purpose of the Church and Its Ministry*. New York: Harper, 1956.

Raines, R. *New Life in the Churches*. New York: Harper, 1961.

Spike, Robert W. *Tests of a Living Church*. New York: Association Press, 1961.

Webber, George. *God's Colony in Man's World*. Nashville: Abingdon Press, 1960.

Wentz, F. K. *The Layman's Role Today*. Nashville: Abingdon Press, 1963.

PART II

Renewing
Understandings of Adult Education

The four chapters of Part II include a description of the basic design of the new curriculum, trends in learning theory, changing perceptions of leadership in adult groups, and a discussion of four issues involved in the reeducation of the laity for the New Day which the church faces.

Chapter 4 shows that mans search for meaning will be furthered greatly by the wholesomeness of the new life-span curriculum which brings to focus the biblical-theological perspective upon his persistent concerns.

Five dimensions of adult learning are explored in chapter 5 and current developments in five learning theories are explained, so that adults may be aided in the growth toward mature participation in the life of Christian faith.

Some emerging guidelines in the social sciences applied in the management of human relations which may be utilized by churchmen for the development of lay leadership are shown in chapter 6.

Is church renewal through a transformed laity possible? What church structures hinder renewal? Can the confusion of roles between clergy and laity be clarified? Can a whole congregation change? These issues are discussed in the light of the plea for church renewal in chapter 7.

Chapter 4

A Search for Meaning

Adults who were educated with a static world view built upon the philosophy of determinism are now undergoing a serious change of thought. As we move into the space age with its new concepts of dynamics, multiple galaxies, indeterminism, and space-time continuum, old concepts become meaningless. New findings by archaeologists in Bible lands make old images of biblical persons obsolete. Advances in human relations prescribe imperative new learnings as man moves much more toward a city civilization in which he is confronted every waking minute by groups of persons with whom he is engaged in continuous dialogue. More automated machines are being used to run machines and do much of the work of the world, displacing men and women and increasing leisure. Can man make sense out of this new way of existing?

Man's Search for Meaning

In the midst of these swift forces that propel our culture toward a new day in the history of mankind some Christian educators of adults have been designing a new witness to the coherence at the very core of reality. In the midst of a situation where many churchmen lament the loss of spirit or the ineptness of the church, they have dared to reassert that men and women, confronted with the choice of retreating from the age of complexity to some more primitive form of security or moving into a new age that demands new designs of meaning and new forms of wholesomeness, will choose life, growth, the risk of adventure into the future, rather than turn back to some luring but false haven of security. These educators dare to declare that men and women can define those persistent life concerns which run with continuity across the life span giving persons a sense of direction for life. Never overcome by the ambiguities or contradictions of human experience, this directive points to a spiritual presence which is cohesive power working toward unity in lives of people. Confronting the fragmentation of the modern cultural revolution, it points to integrity in man and intention in history that are the fruit of man's awareness of and relation to God. Unlike some doctors of the mind, it does not absolutize the irrational. Rather it summons men and women toward a new kind of wholesomeness that restores the true quality of selfhood, reestablishes the dimension of depth to life, and reaffirms the superiority of meanings over ideologies.

A Design for Curriculum

Today's adults represent a large segment of persons whose minds are waiting to be stimulated by the realm of meanings and values. Schooled in a period of rapidly expanding technological development, trained in a mechanized and militarized world, they have been saturated with a "how-to-do-it" culture. The job of the Christian educator is to take these well-trained persons and to enable them to ask the questions, "Why?" "Why am I here?" "What does it mean to be human?" "What is the purpose of life?" They need to rediscover values and beliefs. They need to explore the great questions that give life meaning. Persons who come to the fullness of maturity want answers to the question: "Was it worth all the effort?"

If the Christian religion is to be presented in understandable form, it is imperative that a curriculum have a design for its meanings that is comprehensive. It must include man's relation to God as creator who is active in human history. It must include man's relation to man so that persons may discover the meaning of being human, the ethical purposes guiding man's relation to his fellowmen. It must include man's relation to the world which manifests God's providence and in which man is steward.

Persistent Life Concerns

This design claims that the Christian faith has meaning for the whole span of life. Its curriculum finds coherence by interpreting the meaning of the Christian gospel as it relates to the persistent lifelong concerns of man. Some of these concerns have been delineated by psychologists as follows: (1) work, play, and leisure (Kuhlen), (2) time (McCluskey), (3) identity (Erikson), (4) interpersonal relationships (Lewin). Other concerns suggested by the planners of the *Cooperative Curriculum Project* [1] are these: sense of destiny, survival, sex, affection, usefulness, power, security, trust, love, forgiveness, reconcilation. If a "developmental task" represents an obligation that must

[1] The *Cooperative Curriculum Project* involves seventeen major Protestant denominations who have banded together to formulate a new curriculum design and develop basic resources which may be utilized by denominations for the formulation of study units.

be negotiated at a particular period in life and whose success or failure influences the future course of one's development, then a persistent life concern represents a tendency that continues to influence a person throughout the course of life. A person may change in his approach to it but the persistent concern remains to be negotiated under different circumstances of life.

The psychologist Erik Erikson points out that a child develops very early a basic attitude of trust or distrust which he maintains all through life. At the same time as he learns to receive what is given, he learns to trust or distrust those about him. This has implications for his relation to the world about him, to other people and to his pursuit of avocational and vocational interests. It has deep religious implications for faith, one's sense of dependency, humility, prayer, and attitudes toward evil. It is a lifelong concern. Hence the curriculum which seeks to interpret Christian faith has something to say to people throughout life. Moreover, persons who are continuously working at the meaning of the gospel for this basic attitude of trust need to communicate across age-group lines so that beliefs may be clarified and supported by the Christian community as a whole. Building upon these continuities, a curriculum design has been developed which enables children, youth, and adults to explore the central meanings of the Christian faith with coherence and continuity.

BIBLICAL-THEOLOGICAL PERSPECTIVE

In presenting the offers and the claims of the Christian faith to adults today, the church is moving from a preoccupation with fragments of Scripture described historically to a view of a unity of biblical faith perceived theologically. It is seeking to help persons view the Scriptures as a revelation of the living God who calls mankind into a living relationship with him through our Lord Jesus Christ. If Jesus had intended that the gospel be presented as a set of historical facts or idealistic principles, he would have written them down, as Plato did. Instead he committed the gospel to the minds of living disciples—learners who believed and acted under their own discipline as they sought to be the living embodiment of his way of life. Today each member, as well as teacher, of an adult class has the task of translating the Scripture and appropriating it personally. "The Word" needs to become flesh in the individual who embodies the love, power, justice, and hope of God for man. The learner needs to be involved in a continuous dialogue between the Word of God revealed by Christ and the meaning of human life as he has experienced it so that it may be judged and transformed by the gospel.

THE PRINCIPLE OF INTERSECTION

The key to the understanding of the new curriculum is the intersection of the persistent lifelong concerns of the individual (trust and mistrust, etc.) and the disclosure of God in the gospel. As man becomes aware of God's continuing creative and redemptive action for his being, he comes to a new understanding of himself, of the realm of relationships in which he exists, of his freedom and destiny "as a self in pilgrimage." From this perspective he can rise above the segmented images of man projected by our culture and the particularized data about the universe described by the scientists that tend to cut persons off from a wholesome relationship with reality. From this new perspective the student can explore in faith the multiple dimensions of reality, as a new being with a new insight into who he is and what he may become.

PERCEIVING CURRICULUM AS A WHOLE

Properly understood the new curriculum needs to be seen as a whole. It is not a collection of segmented study units. Rather it is a comprehensive, inclusive, interrelated complex of meanings, experiences, interpretations, and relationships that permeated the life span. Symbolically, the curriculum may be viewed as a circle and the areas of scope as vantage points around the perimeter. From each focal point we get different views of the same reality. This way of viewing the scope of the curriculum may pose a serious problem for scientific thinkers who have been taught to view reality particularistically. Such diverse thinkers as Maslow in psychology and Tillich in theology indicated clearly that participation in the life of faith requires a wholistic self-image as well as the ability to be related to God with one's whole being. From this perspective, *scope* encompasses what God has revealed and is continuously revealing to man for his redemption in the whole field of his relationships—God, man, nature, and history.[2] These are the church's educational concerns.

THE OBJECTIVE

The central core of meanings and experiences are held together by the objective. It is coterminous with the purpose of the church. As Christian educators come to look upon the laity as the church gathered for worship, study, and fellowship, scattered for witness, service, and mission, a singularity of purpose becomes more apparent. The objective of Christian education is to help

all persons be aware of and grow in their understanding of God, especially of his redeeming love as revealed in Jesus Christ, and that they respond in faith and love—to the end that they may know who they are and what their human situation means, increasingly identify themselves as sons of God and members of the Christian community, live in the spirit of God in every relationship, fulfill their common discipleship in the world, and abide in the Christian hope.[3]

This inclusive objective summons men and women to grow toward the fullness and wholesomeness of the maturity that we find in Christ Jesus, our Lord. Both the situation of which we

[2] Cf. *Design for Methodist Curriculum*, p. 13.
[3] *Ibid.*, p. 11.

are a part and the claims inherent in churchmanship demand this singular aim if the church is going to be relevant in our time.

The Structure of Curriculum

Traditionally adult curriculum has been based upon four major types of structure:
(1) religious subjects
(2) broad fields of interest
(3) living issues
(4) problem-centered approaches

The *religious-subjects* approach was most widely circulated in the international lesson series. Here a limited number of biblical passages was selected which usually focused on one religious topic. The subjects may have been chosen with little or no idea of the psychological readiness of adults to study them or of their significance for adults. They were built upon a general scheme that moved through a study of the Bible in a six-year cycle.

The *broad-field* approach has been developed by some denominations in series of books for study that include many disciplines and practical concerns of Christian faith and life.

The *living-issues* approach was developed for Methodists in the adult fellowship series. It investigated the social, ethical, and international issues that affect our lives today. It portrayed the relevance of Christian beliefs and values to the choices which adults confront. Living through so many revolutions with innumerable choices creates an impression of rootlessness in the minds of adults who use this series exclusively.

The *problem-centered* approach has been developed by many churches through the use of community forums. These range in interest from local issues to international crises. Sometimes specialized concerns of older adults have been considered.

Although these structures have served the educational needs of adults in the past, there is a need for new structures consistent with the philosophy of wholeness implied by the areas and built upon the persistent life concerns of adults today.

AREAS OF CURRICULUM

A curriculum for adults today must offer a wide variety of study opportunities, so that adults who come to the Christian community with a wide range of interests and concerns may grow toward maturity with freedom and flexibility. The formulators of the curriculum have designated five major areas as inclusive and comprehensive dimensions of the scope. Each area encompasses distinctive meanings to be understood as well as experiences in which to participate. These areas are not deposit boxes for subject matter, rather each represents a clear way of looking at the total. God's continuing disclosure to man, man's search for the meaning of his existence, new life in Christ, the involvements of lifelong discipleship, and life in the Christian community represent definite focuses from which a student may confront the divine, natural, and human dimensions of reality in the light of the gospel. Moreover, each area provides a comprehensive view of the entire curriculum so that an understanding of any one area should enable a person to envision the whole. The *Design for Methodist Curriculum* summarizes it: "(1) all areas together comprehend the scope; (2) each area reflects all elements of scope [man's relation to God, man, and the world]; (3) each area envisions something to learn about and something to participate in." [4] These areas have each been tested and found not to be sealed off from one another, but rather to be flowing in thought and experience into all of them.

The five areas of scope are delineated as follows:
  —*life and its setting*, the meaning of life, of being human,
    of our history, of the space-time order;

[4] *Ibid.*, p. 16.

—*the reality of God,* the meaning of God's continuing disclosure, the person and work of Christ;

—*the new life in Christ,* the meaning and experience of continuing redemption, man's response to God, inner witness to the life of faith, the work of the Holy Spirit;

—*vocation,* the meaning and experience of discipleship, the outward witness to the call of God in all relationships;

—*the church,* the meaning and experience of Christian community, the life, history, and mission of the church as persons participate in its life work.

From these mutually interrelated areas the whole scheme of meanings and experiences may be utilized in sequences that will provide guidance for adults toward maturity with flexibility and openness.

Life and its setting is the perspective from which the meaning and significance of human existence is viewed. What does it mean to be a human being? What is the origin, meaning, and destiny of the time-space universe in which we live? Is there meaning to human history? Obviously this brings into focus areas such as creation, man, his relationship to the world and to his fellowmen, the concept of eternal life, ways in which we continuously negotiate our interpersonal relationships, the meaning of human history, and eschatology. And many questions arise: What is the meaning of the universe? How do I get a sense of my identity and destiny? What does it mean to be a human being? Why does God allow people to suffer or to be plagued by injustice? Is there any real hope for the future of mankind? These persistent life concerns are viewed in the light of the long perspective of God's self-disclosure through the Bible and the Christian faith.

The reality of God is a point of faith from which the Christian life and the meaning and experience of God's continuing revelation are explored. It focuses attention upon God's modes of action, the ways in which he reveals himself, and his will to mankind. It seeks to comprehend the nature and meaning of the gospel; the relation of revelation to reason; God as creator, redeemer, life-giving spirit; the person and work of Christ. It enables the student to face such issues as: How does God reveal himself to man? Why do I have any need for God? What are the criteria by which the Christian views truth? How does God give unity to my life and experience? In a scientific world, what do we believe about God?

The new life in Christ is the third perspective of this curriculum. Here the focus is upon man's personal response to God's continuing redemption, the inner guidance and promptings of the Holy Spirit, the ways in which we may become a "new man in Christ." Our thinking is directed toward the doctrines of sin, grace, of salvation, of the interpretation of the new man in Christ, its implications for interpersonal relations, stewardship, growth, and perfection. The inquiring adult raises questions about such issues as: Why do I feel so alone and cut off from my fellowmen? What does it mean to be saved? What is worth living for? Why do good people suffer? What does it mean to be free? How can Christ help me change? What is "a new man in Christ" like? What does it mean to mature as a son of God? What does it mean to be a Christian?

Vocation is the next vantage point from which the Christian faith examines the areas of personal, social, and service relationships. Here we are looking at the way in which to make manifest our discipleship in Jesus Christ. We view our concerns about the kingdom of God, Christian personal and social ethics, the concept of vocation, the Christian view of work and leisure, the role of the church in the work of the world, the stewardship of our talents and our natural resources. Here we confront such persistent issues as: How shall I choose and perform my work? Should I serve my neighbor? How do I do it best? How can a

Christian contribute to the decisions that are being made at home, at the church, in the community? What is my responsibility to witness to my beliefs in politics, business, interracial and interfaith relationships? How can I maintain freedom, inner integrity, and creativity amid the pressures to conform in society?

The church is the fifth perspective from which to look at the Christian community, its mission and work in the world. The meaning of the church, membership therein, its mission, worship, teaching, preaching, outreach, service, witnessing, healing are explored, as well as the use of the Bible by Christian persons. It focuses on such issues as the mission of the church in our world. How does the Christian community help persons overcome feelings of alienation? Can the church be renewed so that it may be a vital force in our time? What is happening to denominations? What is the meaning of the emerging ecumenical church?

These five vantage points are inclusive, overlapping, and interrelated. They represent changing perspectives from which we may review and reassess the Christian faith and life in the light of our changing experiences, our deeper understandings of the meaning of the faith, and our sensitivity to the leading of the Holy Spirit who guides us into God's new age.

Levels of Participation

The high rate of mobility among adults makes it imperative today for churches to have foundational curriculum resources for newcomers that will enable them to understand the core of meanings of the Christian faith. In these orientation studies adults need to be guided toward the reference points in man's search for a meaningful faith, new understandings of the Bible, the church and its mission, and the ways Christians reflect upon life and their decisions. Without this guidance people become confused or settle for participating in the church on a social basis. Through a good orientation program they can develop understanding and responsible participation in the life, witness, and service of the church. This kind of orientation takes time. It cannot be done in four easy lessons. It needs to be given a place of preeminence in the program of the church.

After the foundation studies, maturing Christians need to be led into exploring a second level of developmental studies in which advanced and more complex dimensions of the Christian faith can be confronted as persistent concerns of life. A series of studies enables them to face the tasks of parenthood, to interpret the meaning of life to their children, to clarify moral choices and enable them to negotiate relationships with other persons. Adults need guidance in bringing the illumination of the Christian faith to bear with relevance upon these changing situations. As they review their beliefs, they are able to share them with children and youth in their search for a more adequate faith. As they realize that the persistent life concerns are relevant throughout the life cycle, adults find a common basis with the child and the adolescent who have the same concern but are working at it from a different perspective in life. This makes it possible for a whole church to be studying in the same area of concern and to encourage parents as well as other adults to engage children and youth in discussions about these concerns, thus reinforcing the learning experiences of all. A child may be striving for that balance between initiative and the control necessary in his contact with others. During adolescence he usually revolts against the requirements of external controls. Later in adult life he develops a sense of obligation based upon need. Adolescent students may be studying the same area of concern from the standpoint of the alienation they feel at the controls of family, peer groups, school and society, all of which make conflicting demands upon them. Their personal needs may be too great to cope with all these claims. They may feel a deep sense of estrangement. They need to experience God's seeking love as mediated through an understanding congregation. The adults who live in the midst of competition and conflict are pressured daily into treating people as things. Through a study of life's continuing interpersonal relationship across the life span children, youth, and adults may recapture a sense of their own true worth and learn the art of dialogue with other persons. As they seek to understand and to mediate their understandings of the reconciling work of God to children and youth in the family and Christian community, they may grow toward an authentic Christian existence. A series of studies built upon the new design can make communication across age-group lines possible, so that the whole church may strive to discover the way of life it seeks to embody and support one another in their efforts to attain it.

As adults face the demands and responsibilities of maturity, they need guidance in churchmanship, leadership, and responsible participation in the life of faith. This involves more than institutional maintenance and serving on committees. It encompasses the constellation of meanings, relationships, and skills to fruition the kinds of churchmanship described in part I.

This series of curriculum studies focuses upon responsible participation in the life of the Christian community gathered and scattered. It calls for growth in understanding of and participation in worship, lifelong study, and deeper fellowship. What has been learned needs to be shared. This calls for learning the skills of dialogue so that adults may communicate the faith which they authentically represent. Through participation in witness, service, and mission, the laity become the church in the world. Meaningful participation in the life of the church includes this dimension of vocation for the laity. Occasionally special groups of doctors, lawyers, farmers, businessmen may meet to consider their particular mission in the world. The vision of God's continuing action through his people in human history serves to equip these mature adults for the work of ministry in the world.

Although young adults are primarily oriented toward studies

that involve making a living, they will soon join other adults in the lifelong quest for the meaning of existence. They need to be challenged with a continuing education that builds up many disciplines—biblical, psychological, theological, ethical, social, etc., which would enable them to cope with the changing pressures, demands, and interpretations of our complex lives with a sense of integrity and purpose.

A third level of studies is needed for many kinds of specialized tasks and experiences in which adults are engaged. These studies are of short duration. They seek to accomplish a specific objective. They are highly structured to include skilled practices. They would include series for persons preparing to teach children or counsel with youth. They might work on the skills of dialogue for use in a coffeehouse setting. They might focus upon informal approaches to leaders of parent groups. They could be set up for choir groups who need to obtain the biblical, historical, and liturgical backgrounds necessary to lead the people of God in true worship. Such foundational and developmental studies which contain prerequisite knowledge and understandings would lead to courses for more specialized participation in the life of the community of faith.

WHAT KIND OF CURRICULUM RESOURCES WOULD SUPPORT THIS PROGRAM?

Curriculum resources need to be chosen and utilized which provide a variety of learning experiences that contribute to the realization of the objective. Units selected in the light of the intersection between present concerns and the biblical-theological perspective, the mental capacities, and the spiritual maturity of the adult participants should be scheduled in sequences and move toward a realizable goal. Random selections that move aimlessly are meaningless to adults. They will not support them very long. Choice beween studies and flexibility of groupings is necessary if a church tries to move from a social-fellowship or

class-organization approach to one that acknowledges levels of participation so that adults may have the opportunities to converse
across age-group lines and to grow with freedom toward maturity.
This requires finding centers of concern and scheduling studies
with continuity so that correlated studies support conversation
across age lines.

The great abundance of paperback books, audio-visuals, television programs, low-cost rental films has now created a new
situation in curriculum resources. No longer does the minister
have a monopoly on biblical or theological knowledge. Any
teacher or adult student may obtain an excellent library of biblical, theological, and ethical paperback books at a nominal cost.
Magazines, teaching guides, student materials may have a more
correlating and referential function. Utilizing resources which
can be obtained readily, a program may be enriched with great
religious classics and the best of contemporary writings. Both
leaders and members can now make use of many kinds of
materials that stimulate continuous reading and reporting, dis-
cussing and evaluating. Likewise incentive and guidance may
be given to the learning experiences of adults which correlate
their resources on the adult level with those of children and
youth, realizing thereby a life-span approach to the learning
tasks in church and family.

Evaluation of Adult Education: Key to Change

All too frequently evaluation of Christian education experiences is done too superficially. This happens when we use membership, competition with another denomination, or ecclesiastical
quotas as a basis for assessing the real outcome of learning experiences. I suggest a different perspective. We need to ask administrative personnel questions like these: What is your image of
adult education in this church? Have the adults participated in
formulating any kind of purpose for their groups? Are adults
expected to teach children and youth but not expected to teach

other adults? Is adult education simply a reservoir for obtaining leadership for other enterprises? Are adult classes a money-raising set of groups, patterned after local service clubs? Has any plan been worked out whereby the goals and purposes of adult classes are brought into harmony with the educational objective stated in the chapter? How is the plan administered?

If our adult education program is to develop persons who are to be the living embodiment of the Spirit of Christ in the community, I think we may develop these criteria. Does the leadership in a church look upon adults serving in the community as being lost to secular competitors or as a Christian influence upon the community? Is the church viewed as a retreat center within which people can get away from the community? as a conscience approving good and exposing evil? as a mirror that reflects back the social values already existing in the culture? as an agency for change in the community? How effective is the church's real witness in the community?

If church leaders set before themselves the goal of releasing the membership to the living embodiment of the Spirit of Christ, what do they expect adults to do in the service of the church? Does the church recognize that laymen have a twofold ministry? Does the church have a program for the study and placement of its voluntary workers? Does this include jobs in the church, in the home, in the community, at work? To what extent do laymen participate responsibly in the decision-making processes of the church? Are members of the church related to community-wide, national, or world-wide problems? Is there any sense of mutual ministry between leaders in the church, in other churches, in churches around the world?

If the administration of a church school is ridged, stereotyped, and lacking in understanding of the meaning of education and the mission of the church, then all change will be blocked right here.

Likewise there is need for each adult class to assess its experiences. If each class can clarify its goals, I think we may begin to assess the degree to which a church has attained them
by looking at some such criteria as these: How many persons
have joined the church from adult classes this year? How many
studies in churchmanship have been started so that adults may
become "the laity"? How well has the class reached out and
helped parents who seek to interpret the Christian faith to their
children? Are there study opportunities for older adults that
would help them face problems of health, develop new values
for living after retirement, and engage in program retraining
them in churchmanship, enabling them in ministering to other
members who may be shut in? What was the scope of the educational program in education for mission among adults? Does
the congregation have a sense of its own mission?

What outcomes do adults perceive in the lives of adults themselves? Is Christian adult education related to their persistent life
concerns? Is face-to-face relationship between adults cultivated
in your group? Do leaders actually study the meanings of the
Christian faith so that they may communicate them in ways
that help adults grow toward Christian maturity? Or do they
simply pick any subjects of their own choosing? Is there com-
prehensiveness, sequence, flexibility, and movement toward
Christian goals in the choice and use of curriculum resources?
Does your church have its own in-service plan for the development of an educational leadership with competent understanding of the Bible and an approach to Christian theology? In
selecting leaders for adult groups, do members choose people
who have a willingness to grow in their own understanding of
the Christian religion and seek to express the Christian way
of life in human relationships?

If some such criteria could be utilized as leaders and members
evaluate the learning experiences of adults, they would know

more accurately where they really are and move in directions that realize the objective.

CONCLUSION—SOME REASONS FOR THE NEW DESIGN

If ever the conditions of the world demanded a reorientation in the thinking of adult Christians, they do it now. Adult Christians need a new vision of reality that gives meaning and purpose to their existence. They need a new self-image that will enable them to reflect their relationship to God without evasion or pretension. Too frequently persons are running away from their true relationship to God into organization—men, sensualism, mediocrity, or conformity, thereby missing the mark of authentic existence as human beings. Through the curriculum we seek to help persons to be not spectators in worship but participators who are working out their right relationship to God as "the people of God." This is the meaning of liturgy. Through the new curriculum adults are being summoned to a lifetime of discipleship wherein a community of students, sensitive to the leading of the Holy Spirit, seek to appropriate the meaning of the gospel for their lives and translate it into language comprehended by others. No longer can we tolerate adults running around this automated, atomatic-powered, highly explosive world with stupid carelessness hoping that they may hit upon the will of God merely because they have good intentions. Our piety must be ordered, our primitive nativism must be brought under the inner disciplines of an intelligent discipleship.

Likewise laymen must recapture an image of themselves as witnesses, as servants in the world, and as persons on mission. As witnesses they are translators of the gospel into the terms which the people at work in the world understand. As servants they wait for the working of the Spirit in the minds of other persons and seek to clarify, to help, to guide, to interpret new awareness so that these persons in the world come to a sense of their own worth as mental or spiritual beings related to God. This we cannot do for them, but God can use us as a channel through which he works with them. Moreover, in today's world there is no here or there. The church is on mission everywhere as folks seek to embody its message and serve their Lord with sensitivity and obedience. The church gathers for worship, study, and fellowship so that it may be sent into the world as witnesses, servants, and on mission. No slick do-it-yourself approach, no facile schemes or volatile emotionalism will enable us to fulfill this calling in our time. Rather, it demands a reeducated and reoriented laity so that the church may be the church in the world.

Chapter 4
Bibliography

Benne, L. and Muntyam B. *Human Relations in Curriculum Change.* New York: Dryden Press, 1951.

Bruner, J. S. *The Process of Education.* Cambridge: Harvard University Press, 1961.

CCP, *The Church's Educational Ministry, A Curriculum Plan.* St. Louis: The Bethany Press, 1965.

Erikson, E. *Childhood and Society.* New York: Norton, 1950.

———. *Identity and the Life Cycle.* New York: International Universities Press, 1959.

McLuhan, H. M. *Understanding Media: The Extensions of Man.* New York: McGraw-Hill, 1965.

Phenix, Philip H. *Realms of Meaning.* New York: McGraw, 1964.

Sherrill, L. J. *The Struggle of the Soul.* New York: Macmillan, 1952.

Tyler, R. W. *Basic Principles of Curriculum and Instruction.* Chicago: University of Chicago Press, 1962.

Wyckoff, D. Campbell. *Theory and Design of Christian Education Curriculum.* Philadelphia: Westminster Press, 1961.

Design for Methodist Curriculum. A Statement of the Curriculum Committee, General Board of Education of The Methodist Church, 1965.

Planbook for Adults 1966/67. (4412-BE) Graded Press, 1966.

Outlines of Curriculum 1966/67, Ed. by the Editorial Division of the General Board of Education, The Methodist Church.

Chapter 5

Continuous Learning for Mature Minds

Joseph Wood Krutch contrasts two interpretations of a line from the *Rubaiyat*. The first comes from a western tale told by O. Henry. A miner who was courting a widow by mail quoted,

"A book of verses underneath a bough,
A loaf of bread, a jug of wine and thou. . . ."

The reply was shocking and terminal. "You can go on your scandalous picnics alone" the widow retorted. The second interpretation comes from Robert Graves who depicts the Arabic meaning of bread as wisdom and wine as ecstasy. Viewed from the eyes of an oriental poet, the symbols depict a mystical blending of wisdom and ecstasy that is a sacrament. From the poet's perspective the western miner was inviting the widow to share in one of life's sacred moments.

This tale illustrates that what adults learn depends upon what they bring to class with them. They hear what they are ready to hear. They understand in accordance with the experiences they have had and their reflections upon them. A teacher is always caught in the tension between his own understanding of the Christian faith and that of his adult students which is in keeping with their knowledge, background, and experience. Leading a group in learning experiences requires sensitivity to the readiness of adults, flexibility in approach, and understanding of the ways adults learn.

ASSUMPTIONS ABOUT ADULT LEARNING

If an approach to adult learning is to be valid, its basic assumptions need to be checked with the best that we know in the social sciences and in biblical, theological, and ethical thought about their consistency and practicality in the Christian adult education enterprise. It must give an accurate interpretation of the phenomena we have observed in our experiences of working with adults as learners. Moreover, the various parts of a learning theory such as assumptions, description of processes, learning tasks must be related to one another in ways that produce wholeness, unity, and coherence. It must enable us to perceive what is happening to adults so that we may lead them in their development. In the light of these criteria we may want to assess the validity of various approaches.

SOME DIMENSIONS OF LEARNING

Anyone who works with learning theory is confronted quickly with the fact that it is a very complex set of relationships and that no simple explanation will suffice. A quick glance at five different dimensions of learning, namely, feeling, cognition, interpersonal relationships, appreciation, and subjective meaning and personal engagement will illustrate this point.

(1) Much learning takes place on a feeling basis in the Christian community. In fact, a feeling of acceptance is quite necessary for learning in groups. When an individual feels a sense of rejection, he may withdraw and his learning may become blocked. Likewise, feelings of inferiority or incompetence may become an impediment. Responses to love, kindness, and openness are conducive to growth and development. Feelings of ecstasy, spontaneity, and freedom are quite essential to entering into celebrations in worship and aesthetic development. The feeling dimension is present in all religious learning.

(2) Building an adequate cognitive structure of ideas and concepts is a basic dimension of learning for all adults. By relating to word symbols and learning how to use them accurately, we may enter into communication with other persons. The mastery of the word symbols in the Bible or theology is an important part of developing a meaningful relationship with the Christian heritage and for interpreting the way one looks at life. One of the continuing resistances to learning that we face at the cognitive level is the tendency of persons to become fixed in their belief systems. When adults are threatened and feel insecure about the future, a rigid cognitive style begins to develop.

(3) In adult life we are continuously brought together in groups. A great deal of adult teaching is related to the ways in which we perceive people and enable them to work together. This involves learning the skills of helping a group move toward its goals as well as maintaining wholesome Christian interpersonal relationships. If adults are going to be the church as they gather together for study and worship or scatter into their homes, their places of work, and their communities, much of their learning needs to center upon the skills of interpersonal

relationships which enable them to communicate the gospel with integrity and effectiveness.

(4) Creativeness, spontaneity, appreciation are all a part of the cultic dimension of the Christian religion. The spontaneous responses to the true, the good, the beautiful are essential ingredients of zestful Christian living. Appreciation of symbols, art, and music are essential to the experience of worship, meditation, and prayer.

(5) The encounters of life involve the acquiring of subjective meanings and their personal expressions. This means moving beyond objectivity—learning about—to hearing the good news of the gospel as a personal word which we appropriate and make our own. It involves changing under its impact and letting the words live in us and guide our decision-making. It involves our ways of relating ourselves to other persons and enables us to grow toward the fullness of Christian maturity that God expects of us in our time.

Through these five perspectives we get a view of the dimensions that are involved in learning the Christian way of life. They are not mutually exclusive. Rather they are interrelated, interpenetrating, and interdependent. They are five different ways of looking at learning. From these five perspectives we get a more comprehensive view as well as a deeper dimension of understanding than if we had approached the subject of learning from one perspective exclusive of the others.

Is a Comprehensive Approach to Adult Learning Possible?

Psychologically, it is possible for adults to engage in significant learning throughout their life span. In his study of the same persons over a forty-year period, entitled *The Gifted Child Grows Up*, Dr. L. M. Terman indicates that the majority of these persons at fifty were doing a better job of comprehending the meaning of factors in our culture than they were at the age of twenty. Many of them were less capable of handling certain problems in mathematical reasoning, but when it came to understanding meanings and values of word symbols, they were more capable of handling them. Here is the important factor to note—those persons who had learned how to learn and kept on learning were the ones who were capable of growing and excelling even in their fifties.[1] This study is supported by the Duke University discoveries in gerontology which found that many people were still increasing in the capacity to learn at the age of seventy-five if they had learned how to learn and kept on working at it. If they had neglected their learning processes through disuse, there was a rapid falling off in the capacity to cope with new problems and emerging facts. Attitude crystallization sets in and people tend to solve all problems with mere slogans. By this process of thinking, an individual can eventually cut himself off from other people in the world. In such a state of "splendid isolationism" he begins to develop serious doubts about himself and compensating phantasies about the world.

BARRIERS TO ADULT LEARNING

If the potential for meaningful, lifelong learning is a real factor in the lives of adults today, what deters them from more vigorous participation in adult education programs in the church? One clue may be found in the ways that church leaders view adults. Acutally adults are doers—workers, citizens, parents. They bring this self-image to each learning situation. When they come to the church for study and worship and are viewed as persons who are to be "told, taught, and talked down to," their image of themselves as responsible persons is threatened seriously. Many of them soon withdraw. Moreover, persons in positions of authority can lower adults' estimates of themselves by

[1] Cf. *The Gifted Child Grows Up*, pp. 358-70.

continuously saying, "They cannot change." By lowering adult aspirations, the motivation for learning is undermined and persons become loyal robots who sit and do nothing.[2] Potentially this generation of adults has great capacity for life-time learning if adult leaders can work with them in ways that support maximum learning rather than defeat it.

A second clue to the barriers that impede learning may be seen in the way leaders view the knowledge and experience of adults. Adults have experiences of a different quality from that of children or youth. Yet many teachers and leaders ignore these experiences. "My, the poverty of my belief," confessed an adult-class member in a personal conversation. "What do you mean by that assertion?" I asked. "I mean that I do not know what ninety percent of the persons in my class actually believe. Many of them have been through the experiences of suffering, duress, and death. They have something valuable to contribute to my life. I would be greatly enriched if I knew what they thought or felt; yet I have never heard them discuss their experiences in our adult class and learned what they believe. My, the poverty of my belief." Apparently the leader of this group had failed to utilize the variety of their religious experiences to enrich their mutual lives.

Adult teaching and learning builds on the recognized experiences of people. Adults need guidance in reflecting upon those experiences, evaluating them from the Christian perspective, learning how to articulate them, and entering into a dialogue with other persons about them. Adult learning is horizontal education; it is person-to-person communication. Each person may learn from others and thus be enriched and supported by the beliefs, the training, background, and discipline of many other persons in the Christian community. The swift cultural changes of the space age demand it. No one master teacher has a mo-

---

[2] Cf. Lawrence Little, *Wider Horizons in Christian Adult Education*, pp. 88-93.

nopoly on biblical, theological, or ethical knowledge and experience today. We need to move speedily toward this kind of responsible participation in concerned inquiry, if we are to have a competent laity who can be the church today.

FIVE APPROACHES TO ADULT LEARNING

Currently five approaches to learning are being made by leaders and members of adult groups in the church. Each is related to the goal which the group seeks to accomplish. Each has merits as well as liabilities. Hence a group needs to appraise each approach in the light of the goal it seeks, the time and resources available, the limitations and disciplines which this approach places upon persons. Only then can they lead toward the kinds of meaningful experiences and commitments which adults expect of the ministry of the church.

1. Lecturing and Listening and Cognitive Learning

This approach assumes that learning is a process of giving people information and stamping the right answers into their minds. The lecturer imparts biblical, theological, and ethical information to his hearers. Usually the lecturer tries to arouse the attention of the listener in order to stir his mind and direct his thoughts toward some prearranged goal. The chief objective of the presentation is to inform and persuade the learner to agree with the belief system which the lecturer imparts. In this manner, he stamps it in.

The thinking process involved in this kind of approach has been twofold. The more classical approach was built upon a process of deductive reasoning. In using it, the lecturer stated a syllogism which included a major proposition, a minor proposition, and a conclusion. The major proposition might have been that all students of the Bible love God; the minor proposition that Mary is a student of the Bible; the conclusion that Mary loves God.

There are three factors in this kind of thinking: the first

is major and inclusive, the second is lesser by comparison, the conclusion is always consistent with the supposition of the major premise. Although there is need for much greater clarity in the interpretations of Christian faith, the limitations of a simple syllogism of basic logic are readily apparent.

The lecturer needs to ask himself some basic questions as he formulates his presentation. What kind of information is basically religious? What kind of biblical or theological language really expresses man's relation to God? Much biblical truth is stated as analogy. How far can we use these analogies today? How much must they be qualified to convey meaning for a scientific, secular, and urbanized world? Can we interpret ecstatic poetry as an ethical principle? Should a leader interpret "liturgical celebration" as history? (Deut. 26:1-19.) Moreover, what kinds of verification does the lecturer depend upon as he presents the great themes of the Bible and Christian faith amid the vast number of forms of expression? Any lecturer who tries to reduce the Christian faith to a set of propositions will probably obscure more than he ever reveals. The factors referred to in these questions are some basic elements to be considered in the formulation of lectures on the Christian faith.

If a lecturer approaches the Bible as a fact book about ancient times, he will discover that it contains many references to places, events, and people which archaeologists may verify through artifacts, but these data are background. The real drama is much deeper and relates to man's search for God and God's disclosure of himself to man. By lecturing about the facts in the Bible one can create a "meaning-barrier" so that deeper values and beliefs are obscured. If persons learn about the Bible only at the cognitive level, an encounter with God who is seeking to disclose himself to them through the Bible may never be faced in a person-to-person confrontation. Mastering facts is a step along the road to understanding, but the task of education is to lead people into personal involvement with God's disclosure of himself to mankind.

A second approach to lecturing and listening is much more behavioristic. It seeks to fence people in through the use of praise and blame so that they will avoid the pitfalls marked out by the leader and follow the open gates through which he tries to guide them into right responses. This process is facilitated by the use of praise and blame. It is hoped that by blaming a person the leader will stamp out the wrong answer and by praising him stamp in the right one. Using this moralistic approach to learning, the Christian way of life usually runs into trouble when we try to rationalize such Christian injunctions as "Blessed are they who mourn."

The problem involved in appropriating this way of learning in the realm of ethics, human relations, and biblical study is due to the fact that there are not too many well-defined right and wrong answers. We hold the great truths of the gospel in earthen vessels. Learning the Christian faith has a personal dimension— identifying ourselves as "sons of God." An objective dimension would obscure the faith. Moreover, active participation of the learner in discovering and appropriating meaning is necessary to understanding and trying out new skills in Christian living.

The communication of the gospel involves more than imparting information or stamping in behavior. It is a two-way proposition involving interaction between people. It takes place on an idea level, a feeling level, and an image level. The apostle Peter caught the idea of Jesus as Messiah during the experiences leading up to the confession at Caesarea Philippi. He did not understand the depth of meaning of this idea, however, until he had gone through the testing in the courtyard, felt the intense hostility of the opposition, witnessed the trial, crucifixion, death, and resurrection of Christ. When he encountered his living presence during the postresurrection experiences on the shore of the Sea of Galilee, his faith became the response of his whole being to the reality of God as Savior whom he had found in Jesus Christ. Today adult learning needs to move from an idea level, in which persons begin to develop some understandings, to the feeling level of decision-making in the context of pressures in our culture, and on to the image level, which is expressed in identification, involvement, and service.

Many adults are denied the opportunity of engaging in these deeper levels of communication when teachers perceive their tasks merely as transmitting ideas to students. This approach to adult learning may create a "meaning-barrier." When a teacher disregards his student's own search for meaning and does not allow him to enter into some kind of relationship with the meanings and the claims of the gospel so that he encounters these claims in terms of his own personal experiences, then the individual student never appropriates the personal meaning of the gospel for his own life. It is quite true that the leader's exposition of the gospel must be faithful to the meaning and spirit of the Scripture, but the response of the adult must be faithful to his perception of its relation to the meaning of life. Through lecturing, listening, and responding, persons can build a more adequate, cognitive structure. They can formulate their own understandings of the Christian faith in ways that make sense to them. This approach facilitates learning at a cognitive level.

2. Decision-Making as Participation

This approach to learning enables adults to become involved at deeper levels of consciousness and engage in significant exchange with others. Helping adults to participate in the exploration of the Christian faith, to weigh alternatives, and to accept responsibility for their own choices, to act upon the basis of self-determination, to attempt to influence the group to move toward Christian goals are factors involved in learning as decision-making.

This approach assumes that adults are capable of participating in a group. Negatively stated, it assumes that alienation cuts one off from his fellowmen in ways that sever him from reality and impede his growth. It assumes that becoming involved in thinking with other persons, of choosing group goals, of seeking to interact with others in ways that help to clarify meanings will facilitate change and growth. In accepting the tasks necessary to help groups implement choices, it assumes that persons will develop responsibility for actions and grow in the power of self-determination. Moreover, it assumes that persons will grow toward wholesomeness better in groups.

The process implies bringing together accurate information and data, clarifying alternatives and issues, bringing relevant insights in the light of Christian perspectives, and making decisions which bring plans to fruition.

In such a process leaders may take the initiative in helping the group clarify its purposes, the processes by which it seeks to attain its goals, establish limits so that persons may know the extent of their activities, become individually more sensitive to resources within the group that may enable them to achieve the ends they seek to accomplish. The leader may help the group in evaluating its own processes so that it may begin to change under its own direction, maintain better relationships, and implement its plan of action. The leader may also accept decisions made by the group and designate committees or persons with authority to set these plans in operation.

Members of the group have changing and important roles. They need to know how to ask questions, seek and give information, clarify and interpret data, test, summarize, and propose actions. Moreover, they need to maintain wholesome Christian relationships with one another by listening, encouraging others to speak according to conviction or faith, support persons in their basic ethical and Christian proposals, seek to become a channel through which the Holy Spirit may quicken and inspire, be ready to reconcile differences and respond in grace to others.

In the midst of discussion some persons try to use the Bible as a support for their preconceived notions about life. They see only those passages which reinforce their prejudgments. After the agonizing death of Jesus on the cross, the disciples found their minds closed to the truth of faith until the Holy Spirit was able to open them again to the eternal values of love, of power, and of the truth of God. The great meanings of the Bible need to be appropriated by us, and our lives tested for their veracities. In this way beliefs that give meaning to one's life may be clarified, changed, and modified as we seek to look at life in biblical and theological perspectives.

Group decision-making may involve some persons in a new way of learning. It may be a threat to their individualism. It may confront them with a maze of interpersonal relationships and tasks to be performed which confuse them. In negotiating these interpersonal relations in the interchange of ideas, a system of values emerges which influences decisions. Tests have shown that decisions made within such face-to-face groupings tend to reinforce commitments and enable persons to abide by these decisions in continuity. Learning to make decisions and implement proposals can be a therapeutic experience as well as a rigorous one. In choosing between alternatives, in behaving in accordance with the ways he comprehends a situation, a person learns how to work with others, to change in keeping with the meaning he has discovered, and to grow toward maturity in the ways he accepts responsibility.

3. Perception as Image Building

This approach to learning assumes that each person selects and organizes the images he receives in terms of his beliefs, values, and personal needs. One of the major factors determining what he will perceive is his self-image. A person who feels basically threatened will not perceive things normally. Rather, he will select from his perceptual field certain distortions that reinforce his self-image. Moreover, each person sees what he is ready to see. Perceptual learning is highly personal. Anyone's perceptual readiness is the product of opportunities to which the individual has been exposed and in which he has discovered personal meaning. This does not mean the person can be manipulated by new external forces, but it does mean that new experiences which enable him to gain greater self-understanding may enable him to perceive differently.

Perceptual learning helps each adult to discover who he is. This process involves the discovery of who he is in relation to the situation which he faces. If the person sees himself as competent to cope with life, he will probably disregard some impressions, alter others, and blend still others so that he may continue to live with enough self respect and freedom from anxiety to find meaning in his existence. This process involves discovering who he is in continuity. If a person sees himself as unable to cope with life, then he will tend to face new situations with heightened anxiety and retreat into hiding. He may try to manipulate others to adventure in faith for him. Either style of life tends to continue across the life span and to become a basis of selecting images and impressions that support this style of life. As Christian educators we seek to help adults accept their possibilities and their limitations, so that they may be the embodiment of beliefs and values that do not overly distort their self-image by pretentiousness or escapism.

The learning theory embodied in the new curriculum is built upon those persistent life concerns that represent man's continuous development within the acknowledged boundaries of human existence as they intersect with God's disclosure in the biblical-theological perspective of the church. It calls for movement beyond cognitive learning of facts, beyond decision-making to identification of oneself and his relationship to man and God. This is a highly internal process. It calls for examination of one's self-image and the personal appropriation of meanings. Images reside within people; they cannot be manipulated from the outside. They are exposed only in a climate or a relationship of trust.

This fact calls for new sensitivity on the part of the teacher.

Through this approach the teacher or leader seeks to encourage the student to inquire, discover, and evaluate his work. He tries to reduce the sense of threat and to enable persons to clarify their own belief or value systems. He encourages adults to discuss and test their beliefs and their ways of behaving. He seeks to widen the perceptual screen of the student by confronting him with men and women who have heard the message of God and responded to it. Through seeing the relation of other persons to Jesus Christ he can help a student envision his own relation to Christ. He seeks to enable each person to change his behavior as he discovers new meanings and values. The leader supports the learner as he discerns his relationship to God, acknowledges what God has done for him, accepts God's forgiveness, and develops a relationship of trust. As leader he involves the learner in testing his personal meanings with those of others, so that he may interact with society and keep his own sense of the "new being in Christ" that he is.

Leaders who conduct groups on the basis of perceptual psychology will find that individual lives are torn up quite frequently by irrational fallacies that run through our culture. There will always be someone ready to tear up any rational set of personal meanings. Some churches are not wholesome enough in their climate to enable adults to work out a growth pattern in keeping with the light that they discover. Persons who have an adequate self-image can cope with this situation; those who do not will withdraw. Nevertheless, this dimension of learning Christian faith as a personal experience cannot be overlooked.

Adults need to move from learning about God to personal confrontation, from learning about the Bible to perceiving what God is trying to reveal to us through the Bible. The exposure of ourselves to the Christian faith in trust calls us to live our lives in the light of God's revelation to us. The way a person looks at biblical truth is as important as the building of an adequate cognitive structure. Much of the language of the Bible speaks in symbols that lead us to the very threshold of ultimate truth which our minds have difficulty in comprehending. Such symbols may elicit rational denials. The cross itself is such a symbol. As we expose our lives to it, the Holy Spirit works in us to inspire us, to quicken us, to deepen our appreciation of the suffering of God for us. As we feel our identity with this symbol, we recognize that God acted for us and make a response in faith to his saving act. These revelations find their way into the depths of consciousness of a person, becoming frames of reference for his meditation and empowering forces behind his actions through significant learning.

4. "Planned Change" Requires Involvement

This approach assumes that persons are dynamic and continuously changing, sending out influences and receiving them. It assumes that individuals under the impact of these forces will be propelled toward goals or repelled from them, depending upon the strength of the opposing fields of forces, the past experiences of persons, and the ability to perceive patterns or configurations that make sense.

The learning of planned change involves persons in a process of diagnosis, experimentation, skill practice, and the application of new ways of behaving in the midst of change. It best takes place in groups wherein persons accept one another and are willing to work together in a setting with a high degree of tentativeness and willingness to experiment. It assumes that learners are aware of the interaction relationships and skills needed in a decision-making process (see section 2). It assumes that persons consider the work they are doing as significant and themselves as capable of participating in a process of change without too much threat, that they possess a willingness to listen to others with openness, and to get involved in a process of change which may cause them to change (see section 3). This kind of learning is more complex than the previously discussed theories. It is directly related to the action-learning necessary for the development of churchmanship and to "being the church in the world."

The learning process involves weighing the readiness and resistance to change that is to be confronted in a given situation. It involves envisioning new patterns of action, trying out new ways of relating to other persons, and testing their worthwhileness in the light of Christian standards and values. It implies imagining oneself behaving in the light of these patterns to see whether he could act this way with a sense of integrity. It includes trying out new patterns of behavior on the basis of the development of a design to which this person feels a sense of commitment. It includes listening to reports of others in the group and concern for the effect of a certain behavior pattern on them. Thus the process not only involves absorbing ideas, reassessing perceptions, examining feelings, clarifying expectations, increasing one's sensitivity to the ways others are responding, but putting forth the effort to change in the light of this impact of forces as one discovers the relevance of the Spirit of Christ in the midst of Christian groups for living today.

Christians who participate in this process need to clarify their thinking in relation to the Bible, the Christian tradition, and the living faith of the church. The great moral law of the Bible as revealed by Moses and reinforced by the prophets has a ring of relevance for our lives today. Jesus Christ who came to fulfill the law and the prophets has set men free to be guided by His spirit. God's realm is a creative force within and a judgment on human history. The student of the Bible always lives in the tension between obedience and grace. The demands of the moral law require an obedience that surpasses conformity to custom in any surrounding culture. Yet man finds he could never live up to these holy and just demands. Similarly God's great sustaining power enables him to begin again in reworking his personal relationship to the divine purpose in human history. Christians who participate in a change process must have a deep identity with history and an awareness of the involvements in history making.

In this context the Christian learner is required to assess the field of forces working toward change and the factors which resist change. He is required to assess the forces within himself that propel him toward change, such as a discontent with the present situation, an envisioning of a better way of behaving, etc. He is asked to appraise his own motives for change, his competency, his willingness to become involved in the process, and his readiness to work along with others to seek desired goals which change implies. He must be willing to support others in their efforts to change.

Leadership in such learning situations must be sensitive to the changes that are taking place, perceptive of new and better ways of behaving, and cognizant of the relevant Christian beliefs. Leadership involves the ability to create a climate of acceptance in which persons may make inquiries, weigh alternatives, evaluate their beliefs, and explore ways of behaving. Leaders may choose with flexibility a role such as encourager, clarifier, reconciler, initiator, regulator, in keeping with the process of change that is taking place. They may enable persons to test the changes they are making, to evaluate them in the light of their understandings and the perceptions of others in the group, and to support persons in the changes they have made.

In the midst of this kind of action and reflection adults can change their relation to persons within the Christian community and to those outside. They can test their ways of articulating their faith as they meet face to face with other workers at coffee break. They can develop a style of bringing Christian ethic to bear on the decisions of groups. As adults learn more about how to effect changes and become more skillful in changing their own behavior patterns, they grow in flexibility and become more capable of coping with life's varied and everchanging complexities.

5. Dialogue and Engagement: Ways of Being in the World

According to Martin Buber, being is life lived in dialogue. It is meeting with other persons as persons. "He who practices real responsibility in the life of dialogue does not need to name the speaker of the word to which he is responding—he knows him in the word's substance which presses on and in, assuming the cadence of an inwardness, and stirs him in his heart of hearts. A man can ward off with all his strength the belief that 'God' is there, yet he tastes him in the strict sacrament of dialogue." [3]

The dialogical approach to learning calls forth from persons a sense of their own unique relationship to truth and to God, enabling them to serve with creativity. It accepts the meaning which the persons have found in life and relates it to the ultimate meaning which Christian educators have found in God. It affirms that the teacher who seeks to structure the belief system of all his pupils may simply end up by creating a "meaning barrier" between himself and the students.[4] It calls persons who are engaged in this two-way process of communication to begin by listening with depth, and understanding the meanings of faith for the other individual who is seeking to know the truth, and then responding with relevance.

The dialogical approach to the Christian faith asserts that God who reveals himself to man in the Bible speaks a new word to mankind, a living word. Jesus Christ is the embodiment of God's meaning for the word "love." Men and women seeking a deeper relationship to God find in him grace that is capable of enabling them to transcend conformity to this world and the captivity of its culture. As persons become aware of the new freedom God has provided in Christ, they become articulate be-

[3] *Between Man and Man*, p. 17.
[4] Cf. Reuel L. Howe, *The Miracle of Dialogue*, pp. 16-17.

lievers who are guided by "his Spirit." Through this relationship they are saved from a sterile solitude of an isolated existence into a life of openness, a search for wholeness in dialogue, and renewal of mind and spirit in person-to-person communication. Their response in faith and obedience represents the kind of living faith that is the expression of the mind of Christ in us. By articulating this faith in dialogue in ways that break through to others, individuals discover personal meanings for their lives which is transforming for themselves and an influence in the culture of which they are a part.

This way of learning is quite essential if adults are ever going to be the church in the world. Through it the teacher learns from the students; students learn from the teacher. Also, each student must learn from his fellow students. As he is able to hear the meaning of other people, he tries to meet them with wholesomeness, understanding, and love. The tasks of dialogue enable adults in a congregation to perceive a new image of themselves. "They no longer think of themselves in terms only of their in-church identity but as an apostolate," asserts Reuel Howe, "as a 'sent' people whose reason for existence is out in the world where they live and work honestly and creatively on the frontiers of human life; as a 'sent' people whose service of God is not in 'church' but on the boards of institutions for the welfare and education of people, in movements concerned with just relations between men, and in the exploration of the responsibilities of Christian churchmen. . . ." [5] As adults discover the relationships in which communication breaks down, they bring these discoveries to the class, report them, reassess them, change their ways of witnessing, and return their discourse so that there may be real encounter between man and his fellowman. In this process the class or group becomes a center of renewal so that

[5] *Ibid.*, pp. 130-31.

adults may go into society to be the church in dialogue with the world.

The leader in this situation recognizes himself as a resource person who seeks to help individuals meet one another with understanding. He seeks to clarify meanings so that true communication takes place in the engagement between man and man. He seeks to help the students examine their lives within the meaning of the gospel so that the words of the gospel become living words, the words which they incarnate. He tries to help students give authentic witness to the meaning of the gospel. He does not seek to have all students come out with the same authoritative answer; rather he helps adults to relate themselves to other persons in the world with an authenticity that expresses their belief.

The outcome of dialogical learning is the training of men and women for action in Christian faith. It is learning to possess the right answers not for the sake of making high scores on quiz shows, but for participating in the life of faith. The gospel is viewed as a saving event that occurs in human relations. It is learned not to be bottled up but shared. "There is nothing more deplorable and ineffectual than an ignorant minister, whether ordained or unordained; but there is also nothing more sterile than the transmission of information without its incarnation in the personal." [6] The result of dialogical learning is the equipment of the laymen for ministry in the encounters in their families, the community, at their work, and in their daily lives, because they are part of the living "Body of Christ."

SOME EXPECTED OUTCOMES

As a result of lifelong learning in the Christian community under guidance of the Spirit of Christ, adults are expected to become more adequate persons, capable of accepting their limi-

[6] *Ibid.,* p. 149.

tations and possibilities as human beings, living with an openness toward the reality of God, able to reach out warmly to other persons, to enter into the decision-making processes in groups, to be the church in their relationships at home, in the community, and on vacation, to enter into new experiences with creativeness and Christian hope, to be capable of entering into dialogue with the world and expressing the living embodiment of the Christian witness that is a part of their own essential being.

Chapter 5
Bibliography

Bennis, W. G., et al. *The Planning of Change.* New York: Holt, Rinehart & Winston, 1961.

Boehlke, R. R. *Theories of Learning in Christian Education.* Philadelphia: The Westminster Press, 1962.

Bardford, L. "The Teaching-Learning Transaction," Article in *Adult Education,* Spring 1958.

Buber, Martin. *Between Man and Man.* Boston: Beacon Press, 1955.

Cully, Iris V. *Imparting the Word.* Philadelphia: Westminster Press, 1962.

DeWolf, L. H. *Teaching Our Faith in God.* Nashville: Abingdon Press, 1963.

Hilgard, E. R. *Theories of Learning.* New York: Appleton, 1948.

Howe, Reuel L. *The Miracle of Dialogue.* New York: Seabury Press, 1963.

Hunter, D. R. *Christian Education as Engagement.* New York: Seabury Press, 1963.

Kidd, J. R. *How Adults Learn.* New York: Association Press, 1959.

Lippitt, Ronald, et al. *Dynamics of Planned Change.* New York: Harcourt, Brace & World, 1958.

Little, Lawrence. *Wider Horizons in Christian Adult Education.* Article by Reuel Howe. Pittsburgh: University of Pittsburgh Press, 1962.

Miles, M. *Learning to Work in Groups.* New York: Teachers College, Col. Univ., 1959.

Terman, L. M. and Oden, M. H. *The Gifted Child Grows Up.* Stanford, Cal.: Stanford University Press, 1947.

Ungersma, A. J. *The Search for Meaning.* Philadelphia: Westminster, 1961.

Ziegler, J. H. *Psychology and the Teaching Church.* Nashville: Abingdon Press, 1962.

ASCD, NEA. *Learning More About Learning.* Washington, D. C.

ASCD, NEA. *Perceiving, Behaving, Becoming.* Washington, D. C.

MTL, NEA. *Forces in Learning.* Washington, D. C.

NARSE, NEA. *How Adults Can Learn More-Faster.* Washington, D. C.

Chapter 6

Developing Laymen for Leadership

The development of laymen for leadership in the educational ministry of the church is a matter of prior concern in each local church. No one can do it from the outside. The leadership-development process is indigenous to the ongoing, continuous process of education within a local church. This process can only be aided from the outside by leaders who may be instructed in certain kinds of information or trained in the art of using certain skills or techniques. The amount of transfer of this information or skill to a local church situation will depend on the alertness of the leaders to see the aptness of what has been learned, and the readiness of the local church to appropriate new insights or skills.

103

LEADERSHIP DESCRIBED

Leadership in the church involves more than a set of traits or the demands of an immediate situation. Leadership involves a comprehension of the gospel, the Christian faith, the traditions of the Christian community to which a person declares his loyalty, and a sensitivity to what God is doing in the world. It also involves a sensitivity to other people which enables one to discern with clarity their personal concerns, to listen with understanding, and to guide them in their search for a meaningful faith. Leadership in Christian education implies a way of knowing that which is qualitatively different from quantities of statistics, empirical logic, or the critical use of language. It involves awareness of spiritual dimensions of life and thought, the search for comprehension of meanings, identification with personal values in the depths of one's being, and decision-making that is influenced by perception of the value-meanings of behavior. Leadership seeks to enable adults to grow in their understanding of faith so that they may express it authentically in the Christian community and in the world.

IS LEADERSHIP INFLUENCE?

Many social scientists and some Christian workers who follow their thinking describe leadership today in terms of influence. As they study groups and seek to discover the patterns of participation, they point out the fact that many forces are at work in any group, propelling it toward its goal or creating blocks of resistance. They indicate that anyone who influences the group in moving it toward its goal is a leader. Thus leadership becomes the power an individual exercises in influencing a group. In a Christian group this theory may help us understand some dimensions of interaction between persons but our knowledge is highly limited. The real source of influence in a Christian group is the Holy Spirit. It gives persons the power to change; it leads them into discerning new dimensions of truth concerning God that could never be contained in quantities of observations about human relations, and it is the source of compassion which restores wholeness to persons, reconciling man to man. In a Christian group people need to be sensitive to the dynamic guidance of the Spirit which surpasses the influence of persons upon persons.

Is Leadership Ministry?

The new emphasis among religious writers on the role of service in the church is to be commended. Equipping persons for the fulfillment of service roles has a long and honored tradition in the church. Both clergy and laity were called to serve and the "order of the towel" was given symbolic significance for all time by Jesus Christ. But we do not clarify the meaning of leadership when we broaden it to include the faithful response of all people to the purpose of reconciling persons to God. It is the clear function of the special ministry of preaching to lead the congregation in worship, to perform the ministry of the sacraments, to speak God's word in the church, and to lead the people of God in the expression of their prayers. It is the continuing task of the educational ministry to provide competent interpretation of God's word, to enable members of the community of the spirit to become aware of who they are as persons related to God, and to equip them for relevant and authentic Christian living in the world.

There are many kinds of ministries in the church. Leadership implies depth of understanding of God and a degree of competence and skill in some particular field of churchmanship. To maintain that all service in the church is thereby leadership does not clarify the meaning of leadership.

Elements of Leadership

Keeping these critical assessments in mind, we can deepen our undesrtanding of leadership through the observations of the

social scientists and the revelations of the Scriptures. Gordon
L. Lippitt, a specialist in training leaders, describes seven basic
elements which a person needs to keep before him as guidelines
for is own development as a leader:

1. *Insight into self*
   —understand his own feelings and motivations
2. *A modicum of personal security*
   —to listen to and work effectively with other people without necessity for self-justification
3. *Appropriate sensitivity to situations*
   —both emotional and rational
4. *Diagnostic ability*
   —adequate diagnosis of causes
5. *Flexibility in one's role relationships*
   —be flexible to changing demands
6. *Rational relationships through application of scientific*
   problem-solving
   —practice problem-solving approach
7. *Self-actualization and continuous learning*
   —the way by which an individual sees himself in
   the world in perspective
   —to learn from experiences, even failures, frustra-
   tions, disappointments [1]

These observations from social science are helpful in understanding the finite human dimensions of church leadership.
They are relevant to the ways adults participate in learning
experiences. They imply such factors as establishing relationships and solving problems. They may enable persons to become
more sensitive to the personal needs of others and more analytic
in their ways of fulfilling their ministries. They may help teachers
be more effective in guiding the problem-solving approach to

[1] Cf. Gordon L. Lippitt, "Elements of Leadership Growth," reprinted from
an original manuscript, 1961, in *Leadership in Action*, pp. 94-95.

learning. They cannot enable persons to develop competence in biblical or theological knowledge. Nor can they lead them into the transempirical knowledge of God. Churchmen who are prone to overwork a gimmick need to be wary of applying approaches to leadership development in areas of Christian thought and behavior where they do not apply. There is much that social scientists can contribute to understanding the human situation, but such findings must be viewed in biblical-theological perspectives.

FORCES IN CHRISTIAN GROUPS VIEWED IN THE PERSPECTIVE OF BIBLICAL FAITH

Like the findings of the social scientists, the dialogue in the Gospel of Mark (10:35-45) between Jesus and James and John points to the fact that one's self-image may determine his style of life and his relationships to others. If a person wants a position of preeminence in the church because he feels insecure in other relationships, he is headed for disaster. External support can never compensate for internal incompetence. Persons in the church need to accept themselves. Paul Tillich contends that the courage to accept the forgiveness which God offers is necessary for acceptance of self and others in person-to-person relationships.[2] In Christian style of leadership all three dimensions are essential.

In the dialogue presented by the Gospel of Mark, Jesus inquires about the ability of disciples to "drink the cup" and "be baptized." These queries have far deeper implications than symbolic ones. When Jesus took the cup at the last supper with his disciples and drank it, he was demonstrating, through this symbolic act, the giving up of his own life. Later he gave it up on the cross. All leadership in the church costs something; persons must prepare themselves to give up a part of their own lives so that the larger good may be realized. They may be required to die

[2] Cf. *The Courage to Be*, pp. 155-59.

to some activities and to some former uses of time so that they may devote their time and energies to the church. This can hardly be construed as self-realization in empirical terms. But he who loses his life in some sensory experiences may find it more completely in a larger realm of meanings and values.

Likewise when Jesus indicated to the disciples that they were to be "baptized with the same baptism" he received, he implied much more than appeared on the surface. Baptism implies dying to an old way of negotiating the relationships of life and entering into a new way that is not life-destroying. When the disciples acknowledged their personal relationship to Christ, they moved into a whole field of forces at work in human history which sought to destroy Christ, but they gained their support from Christ who bore derision, suffered the impact of personal and collective sins, and overcame them by rising to a new form of embodiment. Thus the call to "be baptized" and to "drink the cup" summons men to enter into a new realm of thought, of relationships, and of dependence upon Christ so that they may be participants in a new style of life. "However loving and sympathetic we try to be, however sound our psychology, however frank and open our behavior, we cannot penetrate the incognito of the other man, for there are no direct relationships, not even between soul and soul," writes Dietrich Bonhoeffer. "Christ stands between us, and we can only get into touch with our neighbours through him." [3] Here is the basis of our relationships in Christian community.

Many people contend that one can assume that Christian perspectives and meanings are present whenever church members gather together. Others, however, object on the ground that the lack of biblical faith is so apparent that it must be brought into each gathering by persons who have been disciplined by it. There is no doubt that adults bring the cares and perplexities of

[3] *The Cost of Discipleship,* p. 110.

the world into the church with them. Many times these personal anxieties deter the work of the Holy Spirit in the Christian community. If the field of projected fears or hostilities emitted by any one person becomes great enough, it can dull the sensitivity of other members of the group to the work of the Holy Spirit. Clarification of perceptions and interpretations is left to competent persons who have exercised the disciplines needed to attain it.

The Holy Spirit is the guiding force that leads the churches into the future God is creating for them. The knowledge which the social scientist observes may help Christian groups understand better the finite limitations of others, but it cannot motivate them to a life of Christian concern nor set them free to be the church in its moral and spiritual dimensions. Sensitivity to and awareness of the Holy Spirit must be cultivated. Much that goes now by the name of sensitivity-training is an exploration into sterile subjectivism. By keeping the Christian perspective focused upon the experimental data on group development, our churches can alert persons to heightened awareness of the complexities of human relationships, but the ministry of reconciliation that Christ has done for man remains the cohesive force that heals man's inhumanity to man. It is the function of leadership to be aware of the work of the Holy Spirit.

IDENTIFICATION OF LEADERS

Any local church that seeks to initiate a process of developing its own leaders will need to agree upon a plan for identifying, recruiting, and orienting leaders. Leaders for learning groups can be identified by the quality of their participation in existing groups. If they show a real interest in the goals of the church, are sensitive to others, and willing to keep learning, they nominate themselves for positions of leadership. By setting up opportunities in which persons may discover their own leadership abilities and want to develop them, potential leaders can be detected.

Anyone being asked to give leadership in the church needs to be confronted personally. There are no small jobs in the church. A genuine confrontation between the person being asked to serve and the administrator is obligatory. The time required, the learning necessary, the tasks to be done, the resources available through the church should be carefully explained. Much of the failure on the part of volunteers in the church is due to a lack of careful interpretation of what is to be done.

The orientation of volunteer laymen to the educational ministries of the church involves a heightened awareness of the meaning and mission of the church. Self-confidence in any task is usually related to skill competence. Hence, a road map of studies in continuing learning in biblical, theological, and ethical disciplines is a necessary prescription for growth and service. Moreover, each leader enters a whole new world of relationships with other persons. He may fear some of them, want to impress a few, and bring a real feeling of warmth toward many others. These feelings will influence his way with others. Helping these persons to accept themselves will enable them to be more flexible in their relationships. One can be a real person without pretense to knowledge. Likewise one can accept in freedom the right of other persons to explore their faith and values in an attempt to find the meanings of life for themselves. Enabling new workers to appropriate the objective of Christian education as their own working goal, creating a climate of acceptance in which they can overcome feelings of insecurity, facilitating wholesome working relationships is part of the process of orientation in any in-service training program.

HELPING LEADERS CHOOSE A STYLE OF WORKING

Each leader chooses a model as a way of working with people in keeping with his assessment of his relationships with other leaders in the past, his appraisal of his own abilities, and his understanding of the situation in the church. If he has been a participant in a highly structured church in which decisions are made at the top and passed down, he will probably emulate this pattern of behavior by announcing to the class what they should believe and how they should behave. If he has been part of a congregational type of church, he would have participated in goal-setting and decision-making. He probably would expect a great deal of participation in this kind of activity, knowing that laymen receive their deepest satisfactions in these experiences. If the experience of church life has been a series of conferences in which decisions were made, tested at various levels throughout the church, the leader may work with other persons to make specific plans of action, submit them to his colleagues for review, decision-making, and implementation through responsible action.

Traditionally, Protestant sects have lifted to preeminence a more charmismatic view of leadership. They have exalted men who had seen a mystical vision or heard some transcendental call. Truly God calls leaders to service through the needs of the world, through providing opportunities for the use of their abilities, through the new creations into which man may prepare to enter. But leadership in the church requires self-imposed disciplines and responsibilities. Overexposure to the charismatic view has produced the authority-dependency as well as performer-spectator relationship in the church. (See chapter 1.) When adults in the church are not involved in decision-making, they become errand boys who expedite the policies which someone else has set. When the decision-making process becomes too involved in power struggles, anxiety breaks down the communication process. In this situation a power group may take over, decisions may be made by this bloc. The few people with ability are placated with some innocuous status positions and apathy sets in throughout the organization. This lasts until rebellion breaks out. Through continued efforts at responsible participation, members can be aided in coping with the essential mission of the church and find mature ways of serving. If this is to happen, leaders must choose a pattern of working with people that makes responsible participation possible.

The style a leader chooses will depend upon his belief of values. If he believes that it is the role of the laity to hear the gospel and obey, his leadership style will tend to be directive, rather rigid, and controlled. If he believes that God has called the laity to exercise their finite freedom in choosing ways to make manifest the Christian life in the world, he will proceed with faith to confront the real issues of life in a climate of openness, bringing the meanings of the Christian faith to bear with relevance upon these issues, and asking people to make their decisions in this kind of Christian context. Persons designated to give supervision to teachers or leaders need to clarify the goals of the church, the style of life by which it expresses its faith, and to help the teachers diagnose the forces at work among the members of the group.

DIAGNOSIS: COMPETENCIES/SITUATION DEMANDS

Growth in leadership depends upon an individual's ability to discover his own lacks in knowledge or skill and then to work out a program for gaining the competence needed. For persons accepting leadership in the church there are areas of knowledge that must be learned, such as: (1) the interpretation of the Bible, (2) the historical approach to the Old and New Testaments, (3) the life, ministry, and mission of Jesus Christ, (4) biblical theology, (5) the history of the church, (6) major traditions in the interpreation of Christian faith, and (7) the basis of ethical decision-making in Christian perspective. This knowledge may be acquired through reading and study. Most church libraries have an ample supply of books in these areas of thought to aid teachers. Most of the classics in these fields of thought can be obtained in paperback for nominal prices. There are recordings of great Christian thinkers. There are movies and projected pictures so that undisciplined Christian thought is now intolerable.

We have an abundance of information from social scientists concerning the skills needed to work in groups. These skills may be learned through practice. Initiating a process of thinking in a group may require defining an issue, clarifying an interpretation, reporting an incident, or suggesting a plan of action. Occasionally groups need to know the limits of the activity, or to have someone bring them back to the topic, or to summarize and facilitate the decision-making. A chart will help a teacher of adults discover those areas where he needs to acquire knowledge of the process or skill in leading a group:

Approaches to Learning	Knowledge of Process	Leadership Skills Needed to:
1. lecturing and listening aid cognitive learning	—forming cognitive structures of religious knowledge —interpreting religious language —reasoning with analogies —clarifying reference points —validating truth or experience	—establish person-to-person contact —identify issues —recognize basic ideas or purposes —give exposition and presentation showing validity of ideas —make application
2. decision-making	—stating issue —clarifying alternatives —interpreting Christian perspectives —formulating thought sequences	—initiate discussion —clarify goals —establish limits —release resources —classify choices —help group evaluate

Approaches to Learning	Knowledge of Process	Leadership Skills Needed to:
	—choosing an alternative —applying it	
3. perception as image-building	—analyzing self-abilities, limitations —identifying with Christian model —appropriating meaning personally —becoming involved in —acting with responsible freedom —evaluating growth and direction	—encourage inquiry —discern patterns —evaluate relationships —clarify images —imagine self in situation —test outcomes of behavior patterns
4. planned change requires involvement	—analyzing field of forces —assessing readiness, assistance to change —determining realizable goals —selecting leverage points —determining plan of action —choosing roles, changing with situation —reality testing —evaluating situation	—create climate of acceptance —be sensitive to change —perceive new ways of behaving —enabling cognizant beliefs —choose roles—clarifier, reconciler, initiator, facilitator, regulator, supporter

Approaches to Learning	Knowledge of Process	Leadership Skills Needed to:
5. dialogue and engagement: ways of being in the world	—listening to persons in world —establishing two-way communication —creating climate of openness and research —speaking to real needs of persons in depth	—learn to sort out kinds of signals people are sending —respond so that you indicate you have really heard what they said —confront other persons in integrity so that you are honest in your disclosures to them —remain flexible, open, and searching in the midst of encounter

As leaders and administrators diagnose the leadership requirements for the educational work that needs to be done, they need to draw up a plan for each leader's growth and development. This may include reading in areas where there is a lack of knowledge. It may require a program of systematic study under skilled leadership. It may demand skill training in workshops or laboratories. All these experiences are now available to church leaders through cooperative effort. As persons participate in them and grow in their own competence, they need to share these learnings with others.

TOWARD SHARED LEADERSHIP IN CHRISTIAN COMMUNITY

As teachers and leaders in the church move to help the laity become responsible participants in the life of the Christian community, the functions of leadership become distributed more and more throughout the group. Hence the role of a teacher or leader changes from presenter of information to that of facilitator

or enabler. Instead of getting his greatest satisfaction out of bringing answers to a group, he may get greater joy out of initiating
discussion, clarifying a problem, helping the group clarify its
goal, setting the pace of work, bringing information that is
needed or drawing it out from others, supporting persons in
their search for faith, and coping with the issues of a Christian
style of life, as well as helping the group assess its way of working so that it may be flexible.

In an experiment conducted in a class at Scarritt College, the
leader sought to involve the members in describing and assuming the shared functions of leadership as they sought to think
through a problem. This sharing was facilitated by reducing
the amount of dependency upon the leader and increasing the
sense of responsibility among members for drawing upon their
own resources. The purpose was to encourage directors of Christian education to set laymen free to be responsible participants in
the work of the church. They were encouraged to create the
conditions whereby persons in the group would have the feeling
of competence to act according to their own self-direction. They
were warned of the danger of losing one's authority and of
having this authority taken over by anxious persons, but this is
a risk all leaders must take in faith depending upon the assumption that eventually persons will learn to act responsibly as the
church.

Increased participation is no guarantee that a group will move
toward its goal. The information recorded on the following chart
describes the way an observer perceived the functions needed in
a group and the ways members responded to them. The data
were reported back to the whole group as the property of all.
No names were listed, but members were identified by initials.
Each person was free to make changes as he saw and felt what
was needed. Obviously when this reading was made, members
were trying to understand one another, trying to hook up ideas
with their own experiences. By reporting this information to

the group, it was to become obvious that they needed to decide upon specific courses of action and begin testing them. By giving this kind of information to the group, persons may change their behavior and chart new courses of action.

Leadership Functions Needed in the Group	Members' Responses		total
1. Setting Goals	J 1 I 2		3
2. Proposing Problems	I 1 M 2 S 1 B 1	J 2	7
3. Asking for Information	L 9 B 3 S 8 I 8	J 21 M 4	53
4. Giving Information	I 13 M 17 B 4 L 3	J 5 S 10	52
5. Proposing Solutions	S 3 L 2 J 2 I 4	B 2	13
6. Asking Clarification	S 4 J 3 L 3 M 2	I 2	14

Leadership Functions Needed in the Group	Members' Responses	total
7. Giving Clarification	L 6 I 4 M 2 S 2 J 3	17
8. Testing		
9. Supporting	S 3 B 1 B 2 J 1 M 1 L 1	9
10. Asking about Group Progress		
11. Summarizing		
12. Evaluating	M 1	1
	Grand Total	169

Local churches need to assess their work from time to time. This process of evaluation should take place in classes and groups as well as official planning bodies. Evaluation is related to the goals which groups have set for themselves. These goals reflect their understanding of the church, their place in its mission, and their perception of the relevant service to be rendered by it. The willingness of members of the group to assess their work seems to be related directly to the attitude of acceptance by the designated leader. If this leader encourages responsibility through group thinking and group action, the members will try more readily to make their contribution. If the members of the group feel that they can experiment in ways that are not prestructured for them, they are free to assess and change in their approaches.

In churches where this kind of climate and approach prevails, leadership can begin to emerge which can envision new approaches to God's new demands so that the church is relevant in this new age.

Breaking the Barriers in Communication

Communication in a group is the interaction process whereby persons influence the ideas, images, and feelings of others, It is a complex process involving the use of words, gestures, bodily posture, etc. It involves listening, reacting, signaling. Communication in groups is facilitated when ideas are understood, the roles and self-images of persons are clear, and the feelings of persons are dealt with as a concern of the whole group. Communication is blocked when persons do not understand ideas, express bored feelings through body stances, reject the role and status of other persons. Much communication is nonverbally expressed in eyes, gestures, positions of body, etc. By observing some of these factors and reflecting them to the group, individuals may perceive the need for dealing with personal feelings that need to be balanced with tasks to be done. If the tensions within the group are too great, the process is blocked. They must be dealt with by someone. The disruption of the communications process can bring about withdrawal, formation of subgroups, or even attack. By stabilizing interaction through personal handling of a problem, confidence can be restored and productivity enhanced.

Much help in the development of leadership can be given by the way persons cope with problems in communication. Leaders must be good listeners. They must learn to hear what persons are asking so that they may respond with accuracy and clarity to their real concerns. Leaders need to be good translators who can interpret the meanings of the Christian faith in language symbols and images which their people can understand. As members learn to sort out the essential meanings of the gospel and exercise their own initiative in participating in the life of faith, they are growing toward leadership. As they learn to share this faith through word, action, and relationship, they are becoming churchmen who embody the ministry of reconciliation.

Growth Through Consultation and Supervision

As teachers and leaders continue to gain competence in their ability to serve, the persons in charge of coordinating administration across the whole life span need to develop a continuing, consultative, and supervisory relation to these leaders. This relationship is built to enable leaders to continue learning and to gain understanding of the whole educational ministry of the church. When leaders become loners, the whole body of Christ suffers. The more the supervisor encourages church leaders to exercise freedom and creativity, the greater the need for clarifying goals and developing ways of working together so that adults understand and support the educational experiences of children and youth.

Scheduling consultations regularly with volunteers is essential to continuity in program evaluation and assessment. Through these conversations the administrator can perceive the way leaders view their tasks, the style of leadership they choose, the understandings of the teaching-learning transactions they utilize, the manner of coping with difficulties they face, and the help they need for further growth. The primary task of the administrator in this setting is diagnosis. Where does the leader need help? Where can this person take hold of the situation? What resources are available that may be helpful in this situation? How may this leader continue to increase his knowledge, skill, and ability in working with adults? How well does he understand the basic educational design and ministry of the church and proceed to support its program?

By approaching all reporting and evaluating in a nonjudgmental manner in a conversation where each party is searching for better ways of working, persons can remain open to suggestions and plan experimentation and change. When the teacher develops too much dependency on the administrator, creativity and initiative are stifled. When a teacher or leader decides to work on his own without regard for the life-span approach to the educational ministry of the church, fragmentation sets in and the whole body of Christ suffers. Without this larger perspective the leader tends to plan on too expedient a basis. These tendencies need to be evaluated in the light of the objective and the continuing process of education for all persons throughout the life span. In such a consultation they must search for the attitudes and actions that show growth toward the accomplishment of the objective and then strengthen and reinforce them. Evaluation should conclude with a sense of the direction in which growth has been made, a reappraisal of the tasks to be done, of the kinds of relationships to be maintained, and of the lines for continuous learning needed by the leader in the future.

SUMMARY

1. The churches have long practiced the development of lay leadership through group instruction by soliciting compliance to goals and requests. Social scientists find that involvement in small groups which determine and absorb goals brings about clearer motivation, commitments, and better implementation of action.

2. If the churches are going to keep a Christian perspective on the problems of leadership, there is need for continuing education of the laity in the meaning of the faith and the skills of churchmanship so that adults may act in accordance with their understanding of the faith and under the guidance of the Holy Spirit.

3. If adults are to move beyond compliance to quotas as the primary motivation for doing the work of the church to the experience of the Christian way of life in their service, then

pastors and leaders must work with them in ways that enable them to change and to participate with responsible freedom in expressing the life of faith. Social scientists have devised many procedures and instruments which they can utilize with effectiveness. There is no excuse for a church to be without its own program of developing laymen for leadership.

4. Many kinds of experiences in the local church increase the awareness of the mission of the church and help persons become sensitive to the situation in which they are engaged. Through guidance, leaders may become more perceptive of their own lacks, discern areas for growth, and set up plans for self-development.

5. Through observation and evaluation persons may be helped to a style of leadership in a church which reflects: (a) basic beliefs about God, (b) ways by which persons grow, (c) competence in Christian decision-making and responsible participation in the Christian community.

Chapter 6
Bibliography

Bales, Robert et al. *Small Groups*. New York: Knopf, 1962.

Bonhoeffer, Dietrich. *The Cost of Discipleship*. New York: Macmillan, 1960.

Claasen, W. Ward. *Learning to Lead*. Scottdale, Pa.: Herald Press, 1963.

Gordon, Thomas. *Group Centered Leadership*. Boston: Houghton Mifflin Co., 1956.

Hendry, Charles E. and Ross, Murray G. *New Understandings of Leadership*. New York: Association Press, 1957.

Knowles, Malcolm and Hulda. *How to Develop Better Leaders.* New York: Association Press, 1955.

Lippitt, G. L. and Seashore, Edith. *The Leader and Group Effectiveness.* New York: Association Press, 1962.

MacGregor, Douglas. *The Human Side of Enterprise.* New York: McGraw, 1960.

Merrifield, Charles W. *Leadership in Voluntary Enterprise.* Dobbs Ferry, N. Y.: Oceana Publs., 1961.

Miles, Matthew B. *Learning to Work in Groups.* New York: Teachers College, Col. Univ., 1959.

Rosenbaum, Max and Berger, Milton. *Group Psychotherapy and Group Function.* New York: Basic Books, 1963.

Tillich, Paul. *The Courage to Be.* New Haven: Yale University Press, 1952.

Leadership in Action, Vol. II. Washington, D. C.: National Training Laboratories, NEA, 1961.

Issues in Training, Vol. V. Washington, D. C.: National Training Laboratories, NEA, 1962.

Chapter 7

Church Renewal and Reeducation

"When the young Francis, with the noose of God already drawn tight upon him, knelt before the life-sized crucifix in the little tumble-down chapel at St. Damiens in Assisi and received the decisive summons 'Renew My Church,' one of those upstream moments occurred," contends Douglas V. Steere.[1] Taking the summons literally, he collected stones and timber to rebuild the leaky chapel. Later he discovered, after clarification, that the interior life of the church must be revitalized. The plight of the church today is similar. "Perhaps the most serious internal

[1] "Spiritual Renewal in Our Time," *Union Seminary Quarterly Review,* Fall, 1960, p. 34.

necessity confronting the church is an examination of our life to see what we are putting before compassion and the search for righteousness." [2] Renewal in the adults of the church is found in the "new men in Christ" whose basic goals and inner driving forces have been transformed from self-centered to God-centered ones. This can be observed in their relations with others in the church, their understanding of and response to the gospel, and in their behavior with their families, at their vocation during their leisure, and in the groups in society to which they give time and effort. Renewal in the church takes place when the purposes of a church are transformed by the Holy Spirit from preoccupation with tasks of institutional maintenance to its service and mission in the world. Here is the primary concern of the church today!

IS CHURCH RENEWAL THROUGH A TRANSFORMED LAITY POSSIBLE?

If the New Testament images of the church give us any clue to the life of the church, then "people of God," "community of the spirit," "Body of Christ," and "followers of the way" all point to the laity as the focus of transformation as they become aware of their relationships to God, Christ, the Holy Spirit, and the Christian ethic—"the Way." If the layman today is as healthy, as intelligent, and as capable as our study of the lay potential has shown, the problems of church renewal shift to motivation and commitment. (See chapter 2.) If the images of church-manship are emerging with greater clarity (chapter 3), there is need to confront laymen with these interpretations in situations wherein decision is required and competence in skill parctice can be tested. Here and there some signs are appearing that point to the elimination of some of the trivial practices of the past and give some clues to new forms of lay ministry in the world.

[2] R. W. Spike, *Safe in Bondage,* p. 148.

"Recovery in Suburbia"

Since Gibson Winter pointed to the flight of the Protestant
church to suburbia, church leaders have wondered whether
there was any hope of redeeming them from becoming middle-
class, white, introverted social clubs. "The cultus of the church
has given way to the manipulations of the organization," charged
Winter. "In place of the sacraments, we have the committee
meeting; in place of confession, the bazaar; in place of pilgrimage, the dull drive to hear the deadly speaker; in place of community, a collection of functions. This trivialization of the religious life has made the middle-class search for religious meaning even more desperate." [3] Can these churches possibly extricate themselves from this kind of cultural captivity? William
H. Hollister of Burlington, Vermont and Browne Barr of Berkeley, California answer, "They can!" William Hollister concedes
readily that the churches of surburbia are captives of culture:
"What often happens is that suburban dreams and institutional
forms join forces and politely do away with the Body of Christ.
The institution may grow in numbers and buildings, but that
does not necessarily mean that the Church is growing in understanding and performance of its particular mission as Christ's
body in that part of the world." [4] Yet he points to the breakthrough made by the church he serves when persons became involved in serious Christian study. Not only are adult newcomers
required to be a part of a communicants' class; they are required
to submit a plan of further Christian growth as they complete
this course. Adult study groups have included the Christian
thought of Brunner, Bonhoeffer, Howe, Trueblood, J. B.
Phillips, and others. As a result, Hollister points out, "A new
kind of layman begins to appear, and an exciting community be-

[3] *The Suburban Captivity of the Churches*, p. 79.
[4] "Recovery in Suburbia," *Union Seminary Quarterly Review*, March,
1961, pp. 292-93.

gins to take shape which understands itself to be a community gathered in worship and study in order to be sent out on a mission." [5] Discontent with putting on suppers has moved them into the life of the city to witness and to serve They have a group visiting the county jail to minister to the loneliness, resentment, and guilt of the inmates. Another group has begun work with students, fixing up a basement of an old building and using it as a theater in the round for dialogues, concerts, and drama through which a Christian witness is made.

Similarly Browne Barr contends that the laymen have not been trained to be the church dispersed. "So before the church can be dispersed, it must be trained, and Christian education becomes something with which the whole congregation, and especially the minister, must be concerned." [6] As an example of training the laymen to be the church dispersed, he cites the adult education experiment in which a series of noonday luncheon meetings for men studying the atonement were held in a section of San Francisco which reached persons in Berkeley who would not have been served through an in-the-church-building program.

REBIRTH OF PROTESTANTISM IN THE INNER CITY

Urban renewal is now moving at a rapid pace in most large cities of America. Housing, health centers, transportation and communications networks grow apace. Not only have hundreds of Protestant churches fled this transformation but those which have stayed find themselves all too frequently with outmoded organizational structures to cope with the changing times. Observing this lack of involvement in the struggle of the immigrant, the alienation of the Negro, the frantic search for tradition,

---

[5] *Ibid.*, 296-97.
[6] *Parish Back Talk,* p. 109.

Gibson Winter declares, "A narrow spirituality refuses to recognize the interdependence and wholeness of life; its concern rejects involvement, and its preoccupation with individual piety derives from the false assumption that the individual soul is more open to change than social institutions." [7] Alternate doses of piety and moralism do not save the whole man from the deep sense of alienation which he feels toward his fellowman and other groups. Yet there are approaches to these situations which point to the rise of a significant ministry by churches in the inner city.

In describing the work of East Harlem Protestant Parish, George Webber points out that Bible study is central. It is not Bible study for subjective "self-understanding," but for gaining perspective on God's dealings with men.[8] It is studied as personal history so that one may be guided into the ways God is seeking to save men today. A second source of revitalization is worship and preaching in which persons find sources of salvation, reasons for their calling, and directives for obedience.

A third source of renewal is found in the fellowship of small groups which are centers of training in the Christian life. These groups are often called "house churches," for they meet regularly in apartments, following the pattern of Acts 2:42, 46. (Cf. Eph. 4:12.) "To take the incarnation seriously in the ordering of the laity involves four interrelated aspects," according to George Webber:

1. "The task of *being truly present in the world*. If God is at work in the world, then the laity must join fully in the life of the world and in that context discover what they are called to do." Each member places a church insignia upon his apartment door so that he is identified as a Christian in the apartment.

[7] *The Suburban Captivity of the Churches,* p. 163.
[8] *The Congregation in Mission,* p. 76.

2. "The Christians in dispersion must *engage in dialogue.*" They listen to the alienation and respond with insightful faith to the needs of the world. When new apartments arise, members move in, listen, and minister to the life of the new community.
3. "The church in the world must *live with compassion,*"—care for persons who may be unlovely but are victims of injustice.
4. *"See with eyes of faith,"* so they may interpret what God is trying to do in our time.[9]

Clearly these descriptions of renewal in the congregations point to the linkage between a rebirth of a sense of mission among the people and reeducation of the laity for being the church in the world as conditions for the revitalization of the churches in the inner city.

In their penetrating analysis of the church today, Morton and Gibbs conclude,

This urgent task of finding an adult, responsible pattern for the corporate life of a congregation depends for its fulfillment on the laity. It is indeed often the minister who alone can set the experiment going. . . . But these experiments cease to be experiments only when the laity who share in them know them to express the way of life they want to live in the church.[10]

Do Ecclesiastical Structures Hinder Renewal?

A second paramount issue which requires some new decisions concerns the adequacy of present church structures to cope with the needs of the world. The swift moving changes on the social scene have made it impossible for signals to be sent to national boards, programs to be formulated, interpretations to be given

[9] *Ibid.,* pp. 139-44.
[10] *God's Frozen People,* p. 124.

to persons in the power structures in or near local churches, and then for responsible persons to implement them. There seems to have grown up what Kenneth Boulding has referred to as a "scale barrier." By the time consultations and conferences are held, plans and procedures formulated, and regulations explained, a kind of inertia sets in that causes the whole process to bog down. Some churches have called in economic consultants to find a way through this malaise, but they overlook the fact that goals are reached in industrial society today through the bureaucratic approach. As industrial organizations get bigger, decisions are made increasingly by small groups of managers. Hence the solutions recommended by their secular advisors may compound the problem of the church. As memberships get larger, decision-making by small but powerful groups tends to increase apathy. Most churches today involve less than ten percent of their members responsibly in developing and initiating the ministry of the church.

THE BALANCE OF FREEDOM AND AUTHORITY

This problem is not peculiar to those churches which have an episcopal form of government. It is the conclusion of Paul Harrison that churches in the "free" tradition find channels of authority to obtain their goals too.[11] In fact, some observers point out that a kind of national establishment is evolving among major Protestant bodies of many traditions which maintains that the real power rests with the people, but on any crucial issue it holds the balance of power no matter who has been given the administrative authority.[12] Yet the crises in our culture break out with increasing frequency challenging the churches at the local level. When authority and freedom to function creatively are not placed close to the centers of responsibility for meeting

[11] *Authority and Power in the Free Church Tradition,* chaps. 4 and 5.
[12] George Hunt, "Sociological Analysis of Participating Communions," *Proceedings of Consultation on Church Union* (2 vols.), pp. 117, 118.

the situation and ministering to the persons involved in it, tension increases. The closer the local church can identify its mission with the real concerns of life, the greater the significance of the church to its individual members. Thus the challenging task before the churches points toward building dynamic local units with enough freedom to cope with changing social scenes and to reinforce them with enough authority to maintain interdependence and lines of communication with their traditional heritage to which they remain faithful while remaining a vital influence within the world.

Gordon Cosby, minister of the Church of the Savior in Washington, D. C., has grave doubts about the church's ability to change its structures adequately for service in the world. "As I now see it and as I now understand the nature of the world, the structures in which the church is contained are irrelevant and simply do not allow the church to be on mission." [13] He is aware that laymen are in the world, but he is not aware that they are in the world as the church. Hence, "the lived-out gospel," the one the world sees imbodied in its midst, is not visible at the crisis points. To the world, that means that the gospel is either unaware or irrelevant. Contemporary man has a deep sense of alienation if the church is not present as a reconciling influence in his life. Cosby feels that its gospel and its mission are not authentic as far as man's way of life is concerned. As one evidence of their concern to be a reconciling influence in the city of Washington, the members of the Church of the Savior have established a coffeehouse wherein they seek to share their own faith with others.

Robert Raines, pastor of First Methodist Church, Germantown, Pennsylvania, is persuaded that structure is necessary for the communication of the gospel, but that each congregation

[13] "Church Renewal: Outside the Structure?" *Christian Advocate* (Sept. 12, 1963), pp. 7, 8.

should be sensitive to the new forms God is creating as vehicles for ministry. In Germantown, Pennsylvania, the church has been revitalized through small groups which seek fresh ways of expressing the Christian life. "Most men in the modern world will only discover the gracious God in and through gracious neighbors, creating a veritable neighborhood of grace in the world," declares Dr. Raines. "It is our task to create such communities of grace in every corner and sector of modern life where a world-seeking community can find it in Christ." [14]

Any assessment of church structures must focus on at least three factors. (1) How well do the structures aid in communicating the gospel throughout various organizations and in the community? (2) How does the church interpret its mission or ministry to persons? Is it building-centered? Does it have any outreach, influence groups, or does it change life in any vital way in the community? (3) Does it have a clear structure of authority that encourages persons to take the initiative as Christians in accordance with the goals of the church and the guidance of the Spirit? Is all action impeded until officially sanctioned? Is the source of authority so confused that an inner power struggle continues, depleting the church's strength? The way a local church or a denomination seeks to answer these questions operationally will determine whether its structures are a help or a hindrance to its renewal.

Any change in structures implies a change in power. A group has power when it can make its influence felt in the decision-making processes of a church. The church has evolved its present structures through years of coping with attacks from without, heresy within, the rise of a culture creating laity in the Reformation, and the manifold spawning of sectarian leaders who found fertile soil on the new frontiers. (See chapter 2.) Today, these establishments are being challenged by the swift-moving forces

[14] *Ibid.*, p. 10.

of social change. Perhaps an analogy from the civil rights movement will illumine the situation. As Negroes in many regions gained power to improve their way of life, they became more responsible for their behavior in many areas of life. Others who did not have their lot improved were frustrated more deeply and revolted more violently. Churchmen working with them ceased the kind of service in which we do things for people and began to do things with them. When this happens, people develop the capacity for using power. Wise churchmen know that power is not distributed from the top down. It exists throughout the church. Programs may be formulated at the top, but any local church can revise the quota, change the time schedule, give lip service to the project and be too busy to get it done. There are many ways to exercise their authority. The problem in restructuring the church then is to help the laity assume and use power responsibly.

Is There Role Confusion Between Clergy and Laity?

A third issue which emerges in any discussion of church renewal through a reeducated laity focuses on the role confusion between clergy and laity. Ministers, some people claim, have so many pressures and demands upon them that they have no time for training the laity for service. The proclamation of the gospel is supposed to be the sole prerogative of the preacher who must be a specialist. Increased discussion of the "ministry of the laity" is said to spread confusion.

These objections are symptoms of a far deeper conflict within the clergyman himself. If he is going to help laymen assume and use power, he is threatened. Today the primary role of a minister is that of administrator or director of the congregation's activities. Any clergyman who enables the laity to accept responsibility for the program of the church knows they will take over directing these activities. They will do it differently from the way he is doing it, and they do not have the same amount of accountability placed upon them as he has placed upon himself. If a clergyman is going to facilitate any change in structure or roles, he must feel more secure than he does at present. Along with new privileges go structural changes that place responsibility and rewards in right relationship.

Any group of laymen and clergymen who desire to clarify the present confusion in "the church" over the roles of clergymen and the functions of laity in performing the ministries of the church need to begin by relating their thinking to three reference points: (1) biblical, (2) traditional, and (3) functional. If the Letter to the Ephesians, especially chapter 4, is selected as a basis of thinking through the ministries of the church, certain factors become plain. Unity is paramount. There is "one God and father of us all," "one Lord" who unites us all, "one Spirit" who permeates and guides all ministries. It is the duty of all who minister to "maintain the unity of the Spirit in the bond of peace" (4:3). The wide variety of gifts to be used for various ministries are given in the service of "one Lord" who is head of the church. Laymen who assume the role of service in the church are thereby obligated to study to know the mind of Christ so that they may be the "body of Christ" that is in continuous relation to "the head." Freedom in the church does not mean doing what you please. To serve in the church is to choose and act in accordance with God's will because we have been set free from sin that distorts the goals of life. Clergymen who were ordained have given evidence that they are ordered in their search for God's will. In this ordering the clergyman finds a deep security that comes from continuous study to know the mind of Christ. This security can be maintained as he exercises his role as teacher of the new laity. Laymen who assume the obligations of ministry are under the same obligation of self-discipline through study. Today this is possible for all because of the wide dissemination of resources at very nominal costs and the increased ability of adults to do so. Without some kind of order the essential unity of the church disappears in the ambiguities of life.

Traditionally, the churches of Europe viewed the ministry as threefold: prophetic, pastoral, and priestly. In America the early churches resembled the state churches of Europe. The opening of the frontier changed the church to a "voluntary society" and the minister became a forceful evangelist who could persuade people in a highly competitive situation to follow him. The westward trek added the missionary role to the clergyman. The growing industrialism and the rise of the city slum gave rise to the social reformer and community leader who initiated settlement houses, institutional churches, and welfare programs. The onslaught of two world wars gave new credence to the chaplain, while the worldwide ideological struggle has given a new eminence to the theologian-lecturer. Amid this vast array of clergy images competing for top priority in our pluralistic religious culture in America, both clergy and laity must agree upon some authentic form of ministry that will communicate with people in our time and have authentic continuity with the past. In those congregations where the traditional roles of the clergy are clearly designated as preaching the word and administering the sacraments, there is need to free the minister from accumulated organization jobs, to clarify with laymen their roles in the various ministries of the church, and then to interpret the mutual relationship and tasks of clergy and laity.

Considered functionally, the church is viewed by laymen as an agency that gets things done. As an agency, it is task-oriented and related directly to other agencies in the world. It is the arena of man's responsibility. His stewardship is defined not only in terms of church management but of the relationship of church and world. It is a lay responsibility to bring the concerns of Christians in the world to the church and to have these concerns considered on the agenda of churchmen. These concerns imply Christians relationships to the technological civilization, highly organized intergroup relationships, and power structures of our secularized urban existence. They cannot be met by retreating into mythology, into the nostalgia of romanticized versions of rural life, or into petty moralisms. They represent the point of encounter between the church and the world. Here the clergyman is interpreter of the gospel to laymen who must translate it into a thousand technical languages in a secular culture. Here the clergyman becomes a coach leading vocational groups of laymen in skill-practice sessions in "doing the truth" so that they may bring Christian ethic to actualization in the decision-making power structures of society. (See chapter 5.) "Our culture is a teleological, or purpose-oriented, culture, and man is the fashioner of purposes," contends Harvey Cox. "We size things up by asking what they are for, and to say of something or of someone that he is useless is about the worst thing we can say." [15] Unless the church can train the laity in the arts of mission and witness, it sends them forth to be useless as Christians in the world. Uselessness destroys one's feeling of worth. Here is the meaning of redemption which contemporary man longs to experience in our secular culture. Lack of this dimension in the life of the church has brought about the anomalous situation in which the clergy must march in the streets to keep the gospel visibly alive while laymen take over pulpits. (See chapter 1.) An instrumentalist culture is a "show me" culture. Any discussion of clergy-laity relationship must refer to the realities of this culture and define the church as mission in terms of renewal for reengagement.

THE EDUCATIONAL ROLES OF THE MINISTER

Many ministers who are taking the educational functions of their office seriously are reassessing their own relationships to the tasks of Christian education in the local church. Reduced to

[15] *The Secular City*, chap. 3.

their minimum proportions, they have defined the tasks of "equipping the saints" to three dimensions: (1) educating all newcomers into an understanding of and participation in the life of Christian faith; (2) teaching the biblical-theological interpretations to teachers in the church school so that they may have an adequate belief and value system for support in their work; (3) equipping the members for their ministry in the world.

Traditionally many ministers have fulfilled the obligation to instruct newcomers to the church through short, simple, preparatory classes. Usually they summed up the tenets of the faith in terms of propositions and the distinctive emphases of their denomination in a brief lecture. The problem of helping persons find their identity in the Christian community and of being able to participate in it requires more education than a few meetings allow. Consequently, new experiments are being tried. In a day when it cannot be assumed that our pluralistic culture supports the Christian meanings and way of life, the obligation to make these meanings clear is of supreme importance. Drawing upon their disciplines in theological thinking and biblical interpretation, ministers are spending more time in study with those persons who desire to enter into fuller participation in the Christian life. In the First Methodist Church at Palo Alto, California, the minister of education, Braxton Combs, has conducted groups that meet for two half-hours one night each week for sixteen weeks. During this time the basic perspectives of the Christian faith are explored as they relate to the current problems of existence. Each evening's session centers upon the meaning of the Christian faith for one's own personal experience. No one is asked to join the group unless he is willing to accept certain personal disciplines and to take Bible study seriously. Each session includes periods of fellowship, of study, of confession or witness, of worship, and the acceptance of service. The results have included renewed participation in the life of the church based upon understanding. This new dynamic has infused much of the leadership of the church. Now vocational groups, having completed the basic courses, are meeting to explore the ways in which they may be the embodiment of the church in the world.

A second dimension of the minister's educational task involves interpreting the Bible, theological topics, and Christian ethic to lay teachers. The symbols of Christianity need to be interpreted if laymen are going to believe in them and conduct their lives in relation to God. There are distinct approaches and disciplines of thought that are coherent with these approaches to the study of the Bible or Christian faith. If laymen are left to wander around in these studies without knowing the difference between a historical approach and a biblical-theological one and the thought forms which support each, confusion reigns throughout the church. Moreover, when religious leaders try to verify the affirmations of faith by the experimental methods of science, they may distort completely their implications for our existence. The minister's primary educational task is the interpretation of the faith, especially to teachers.

A third dimension of the educational ministry of the clergy is training the laity for dialogue and witness in the world. If we are to take seriously the mission of the church in the world, our education must develop the laity to be effective witnesses. Approaches are now being made through vocational groups, small groups meeting in homes, and concern groups which are usually related to a particular concern. In Tenafly, New Jersey, a church brought together periodically a group of salesmen to consider "Our case, e.g., Christian Approach to Sales Ethics." At North Broadway Methodist Church in Columbus, Ohio, a group of laymen studied "Prayer" and visited the same persons in wards of the hospital over a period of time to discern whether intercessory prayer made any difference. In Alexandria, Virginia, a group of persons deeply concerned about peace met to see whether they could find any breakthroughs in the present web of hostilities, any new perspectives and approaches to old entanglements and relationships. In Monroe, Louisiana, Dr. Ben Oliphant reported that many adults were meeting in small groups informally to help people with their own problems, to review issues in the community and plan some action, to review movies or television shows and appraise them in the light of Christian values. These groups had therapeutic, educational, and witnessing value. They were an expression of the church in dialogue with the world.

The multiple expressions of the church's life in the world indicate the variety of situations to which every congregation must witness. Whether or not they are aware of it, as soon as people leave the church doors they are witnesses in the world. If they are going to be representative of the life of the church, the minister needs to give more attention to the training of the educational ministry of the church.

Here are three distinct areas in which ministers may make a real contribution to the educational life of the church. They require a working knowledge of the Bible and the Christian faith. They do not require a mastery of teaching techniques, although a basic understanding of people and the way they learn will help the minister in the ways he communicates with them. If the roles of a clergyman as educator can be clearly defined and the obligations of the laity agreed to, much of the present confusion over the work of clergy and laity can be overcome.

CAN A WHOLE CONGREGATION CHANGE?

Many churchmen who have been sending adults to leadership development projects for years are reassessing their expectations concerning the effectiveness of these persons when they return. Like a cup of water that is poured back into the sea, their influence for change often seems to be lost in the mass of the congregation. Granting that the experience was good for the individual, its lasting effect on the life of the church seems to be: so what? Consequently, church leaders are devising experiences wherein the whole congregation can be involved in an effort to bring about renewal.

PARISH LIFE CONFERENCES

The Episcopal Church has found the Parish Life Conference a faith-renewing experience for clergy, teachers, and laity alike. It is an attempt to communicate the faith in a conference setting so that it will be understood in terms of relationships as well as ideas. It is an experience of the faith as well as a verbal encounter with its meaning. It is an attempt to help a local parish rediscover, clarify, and implement the faith that it seeks to embody.

The conference may be held within a local church or among minimum groups of five people from four to six parishes. After they have become acquainted and name tags have been distributed to identify each person, the conferees are asked to pair off in twos. They are then asked to explore the first question, "What is the purpose of your parish church?" Searching, defining, and sharing continues. Later in the conference, the delegates face the question, "What is the deepest need of man?" When the members are involved in this discussion, the leader begins to introduce cases which enable them to test their beliefs and actions and to assess their adequacy. Through this process the participants begin to change both their ideas and relationships.

After they return home, the churches or groups visit one another to evaluate the changes they have been able to bring about as a result of the Parish Life Conference. They assess new factors, problems, and possibilities. Such a conference does not pretend to give a magic formula for renewal, but it does set in motion the expectation and process of change.

RETRAINING OLDER ADULTS FOR CHURCHMANSHIP

No church can hope to bring about renewal to any great degree if it does not take seriously the task of retraining older adults for senior churchmanship. A process of change in the church requires that leaders change along with their members, otherwise they will freeze the whole process throughout the church. This is especially true of persons working with older adults. If they are not expected to change, the process becomes arrested right then and there. Older adults can change their values, beliefs, relationships, and skills, but they want places of significance that give them a sense of worth as they participate in the life of the church. The actor becomes director, then producer. The businessman may move from sales to management to an advisory position. Likewise older adults need a whole new set of significant roles in the church in keeping with their maturity, experience, wisdom, and energy. They cannot be anesthetized with sentimentalism. As the span of work years is lessened and the length of life increased, they must be retrained for service that makes a worthwhile contribution to the church.

A few samples of volunteer service opportunities may indicate how older adults can be made to feel that they are contributing to the life of the church:

—writing a history of the church and interpreting it (dramatically, pictorially, etc.) to all newcomers in the church;

—directing the center of continuing education of older adults. St. Luke's Methodist Church in Oklahoma City has a comprehensive program of lifelong education presenting opportunities at many levels with guidance for all;

—tutoring school dropouts. This program has had significant results in Nashville, Tennessee;

—starting a referral service at the church for persons who need help—legal, medical, housing, jobs, etc.;

—learning new skills to work with persons who are handicapped, homebound, or hospitalized;

—acting as hostesses in service agencies of the community;

—surveying housing needs of older adults who dwell in overcrowded city apartments and developing consultations with owners or government officials to create better living conditions for them;

—maintaining a church library and improving its utilization by church leaders;

—participating on consultative committees that will study and report to the program-planning agencies of the church;

—participating in the mission of the church in ways that enable them to share the new life they have received with adults around the world who are caught in poverty and disenchanted with life.

God's gift of longer life has bestowed upon the church a new potential. If leaders choose to ignore or spurn it, the church has no message to adults concerning a life in which one can realize his *full* possibilities. The time is NOW for the fulfillment of all potentialities which are truly one's *self*.

CONCLUSIONS

The answers formulated by a church to the four issues raised in this chapter determine the outcome of any reeducation of the laity for churchmanship. If there is no expectation of renewal, the motivation for responsible churchmanship has been stifled. Many churches guided by the Holy Spirit have gained a new vision of the potential of the laity to be the church. They have reconstructed their educational ministry to all adults to participate meaningfully in the life of Christian faith. Clergymen have found their new educational roles worthy of the mission of the church as they "equip the saints for ministry."

Awakening from their long slumber as spectators, congregations are finding the new stimulus to be Christians in all of life's relationships a source of renewal, a challenge to lifelong discipleship, and a way of maturing that has eternal dimensions.

Chapter 7
Bibliography

Ayres, Francis O. *The Ministry of the Laity.* Philadelphia: Westminster Press, 1962.

Barr, Browne. *Parish Back Talk.* New York: Abingdon Press, 1962.

Bonhoeffer, Dietrich. *The Cost of Discipleship.* New York: Macmillan, 1960.

Boulding, Kenneth. *The Organizational Revolution.* New York: Harper & Bros., 1953.

Campbell, Ernest Q. and Pettigrew, Thomas F. *Christians in Racial Crisis.* Washington, D. C.: Public Affairs Press, 1959.

Cox, Harvey. *The Secular City.* New York: Macmillan, 1965.

Gibbs, M. and Morton, T. R. *God's Frozen People.* Philadelphia: Westminster Press, 1965.

Grimes, Howard. *The Rebirth of the Laity.* Nashville: Abingdon Press, 1962.

Harrison, Paul M. *Authority and Power in the Free Church Tradition.* Princeton: Princeton University Press, 1959.

O'Conner, E. *The Call to Commitment.* New York: Harper, 1963.

Raines, R. *Reshaping the Christian Life.* New York: Harper, 1964.

Spike, R. W. *The Freedom Revolution and the Churches.* New York: Association Press, 1965.

———. *Safe in Bondage.* New York: Friendship Press, 1960.

Webber, G. W. *The Congregation in Mission.* Nashville: Abingdon Press, 1964.

———. "Renewal in the Churches." *Union Seminary Quarterly Review,* XVI, No. 3, March 1961.

———. "The Laity Renaissance," *Religion in Life,* Winter, 1961-62.

Winter, Gibson. *The Suburban Captivity of the Churches.* New York: Doubleday, 1961.

PART III

Reconciling Relationships —
The Church in the World

Any program of educating the laity to be the church includes such goals as witness, service, and mission in the world. This is the arena wherein the laity confronts secular life in industry and leisure (chapter 8), in home and school (chapter 9), and in the power structure and communication systems that determine our common destiny (chapter 10).

Ever since Dietrich Bonhoeffer returned to Nazi Germany to oppose tyranny in the face of martyrdom, Christians have been awakened anew to the question: How and where shall the church be in the world? It must accommodate the biblical view of the universe to the truth of modern astronomy and physics, contends John A. T. Robinson. It must be a servant waiting upon the action of God in human life and enabling persons to respond in faith, says Gibson Winter. It must be at the point of intersection where the influence of history affects man, and where man influences history, asserts Harvey Cox.

Whose voice shall we hear? Who has the wisdom to guide the church amid the complexities of our swiftly changing world? A search for answers leads to many ambiguities in the changing scene of work and leisure. The challenge of an affluent and automated society calls for a reassessment of the vocation of the laity so they may articulate the Christian witness in the decision-making bodies in the halls of production, commerce, and advertising, and become creators of a new culture during the increasing hours of leisure.

The church is also in the world as sustainer of persons, interpreter of meanings, and champion of love in human relationships that enables persons to find their true selfhood. Through families it helps them to appropriate the gospel for their lives and relate its beliefs with relevance to the culture they confront.

Being the church in the world requires an awareness of what is taking place in our time. Perceived from the vantage point of a Christian view of history, here is the burden of the dialogue outlined in chapter 10. If the mission of the church in the world is to be relevant to the power structures that determine our common destiny, Christian participation and involvement in the moment of realized history must be seen in the light of God's continuing creation. Christians are called to "be there" to minister in ways that influence the future so that God who acts in history may bring his realm to realization in the affairs of men.

Chapter 8

The Time of Our Lives

One of the unique qualities of man is his consciousness of time. Anyone who has taken the journey down the trail in the Grand Canyon to the chiseling waters of the Colorado River, is confronted with geological exposures that record the earth's past for over a million years. This past reveals those species of nature which were stamped out by their contemporaries, leaving only a thin strand of encrusted evidence. Other species were able to adjust to one another in ways that sustained life for longer periods. They left thicker deposits of encrusted residues which stand as silent monuments to the way of life in the seas of hundreds of thousands of years ago. As the slashing river cut its way through the tilted Kaibab mountains, it revealed in the variety of rocks laid bare the forces and the forms, the volcanoes

147

and the seas at work in molding the surface of the earth that sustains our life. As one passes through stratum after stratum, he is entranced by this record in retrospect of changes by the chronicler of time.

THE MEANING OF TIME FOR PERSONS

The vision of past epochs has meaning for man in the present and is determinative in all our lives. Life is not predetermined by events that have gone before, albeit these occurrences set the conditions for our lives. The decisions and the influences set in motion by Moses and Pharaoh, Jesus and Pilate, Paul, Augustine, Charlemagne, Luther, Lincoln, Madame Curie, Albert Einstein —all have been forces in human history that have an effect upon the events of the present. Moreover, you and I are temporal events also. What we do with the beliefs, values, knowledge, and conditions that are our heritage may alter what we choose to do with the present moment. But man has finite freedom enough to ask questions and build new structures. The laws of the universe which once we perceived as absolute turn out, upon closer examination, to be statistical probabilities. What each individual does with the time of his life depends upon the transformation he undergoes through the influences and opportunities which he utilizes to set new configurations of meanings in motion. Change is continuous, but the way in which we express the many potential responses in any situation depends upon our use of the time present.

LONGER LIFE—SHORTER WORK YEARS

In recent years the improvements in health habits and medicine have increased greatly the length of our years. The swiftness with which we can now move through space enables us to accomplish as much in one day's work as we could do formerly in three or four days. In a sense this lengthens the work years of our lives. Moreover, the swift changes that occur during a lifetime may be compared to those within five-hundred-year periods of the Middle Ages. If the decisions and forces we set in motion today influence the whole future of mankind, indeed, man's consciousness of time, past, present, and future, they place new obligations upon us for perceiving the whole of life, planning for the full development of our potentialities, managing relationships, and making those contributions to the life of mankind that foster maximum spiritual, mental, moral, and social development for all.

Recently a vocational-guidance counselor startled me by saying that it would soon become possible to advise young persons to take the first twenty-five years of their lives to prepare for work, the second twenty-five years as the time for earning a living through employment, the next twenty-five years to make their contribution to society or culture while being supported by pensions, investments, insurance, social security, etc., and the last twenty-five years in retirement. Although the time of our lives may not fit into such neat categories, the situation to which he points is coming rapidly upon us. Automation is shortening the work years while the time for leisure increases. Our technological society requires highly skilled workmen, yet machines that control machines accelerate production. This has created a situation with which our society and our Christian ethics are not prepared to cope.

AUTOMATION CHANGES THE NATURE OF WORK

As the industrial revolution of our time enters its third phase, it is changing greatly the work life of man. When mechanization was introduced in the eighteenth century and created the factory system, about ninety-five percent of our work was done by the muscle of man, about five percent by machine. Today it is almost reversed. The beginning of the twentieth century, when assembly line and mass production enhanced the manufacturing of goods in abundance, sent us searching vigorously for new forms of power. Today we measure the power used by man in a lifetime not in terms of horses but in terms of energy given off by the rays of the sun.

In the third phase of the industrial revolution machines have changed the factory system into a single, unified, automatically controlled unit. It synchronizes every phase of the production process, so that an IBM card can be dropped into a computer at one end and a new automobile with all parts assembled in working order roll off the line at the other. Increasingly machines will run machines.[1]

In fact it was the considered opinion of Norbert Wiener, the founder of the science of cybernetics, that in structuring the machine to perform certain functions previously done by men through conditioned reflexes or by a process of analogical reason, men could be freed from tedious, complex, calculating chores for more creative activity.[2] Dr. Wiener saw little difference between machines of metal and machines of flesh if either was little more than cogs and rods and levers in an organization.[3] "There is one quality more important than "know-how" and we cannot accuse the United States of any undue amount of it," he writes. "This is 'know-what' by which we determine not only how to accomplish our purposes, but what our purposes are to be." [4] It was man's work to ask the machines the right questions.

It was part of the American dream that the increase of machine production would free some men from long hours of toil. In this new freedom from toil, man would be able to develop as a human being. It has not happened. Executives are putting in fifty-five hours a week to keep workers going for thirty-five to forty hours. Many laborers whose jobs are cut to thirty-five hours a week get

---

[1] Cf. W. Buckingham, *Automation,* p. 14.
[2] *The Human Use of Human Beings,* pp. 57, 63, 64.
[3] *Ibid.,* p. 185.
[4] *Ibid.,* p. 183.

a second job to do more work. Our work force uses women in about forty percent of the jobs. Work consists of tending the machines, starts when they start, stops when they stop. Instead of increasing free time, the bewitching whirl of the machine has bound us to the clock.

OUR ETHIC CREATES GUILT IN LEISURE

We are a work-oriented society that makes anyone feel guilty when he is not working. This anomalous situation prevails at a time when we have developed the means of production to free man to create a new quality of life, enrich his culture, find depth of meaning for his existence. Why? I venture the opinion that the problem does not lie in the system of production but largely in the Puritan ethic which the churches inherited and continue to support.

In the Middle Ages poverty, ignorance, and disorganization abounded. The life of the serf was hard and precarious. Monks joined in manual work as acts of self-purification or as acts of charity toward others. Yet they reserved intellectual work, contemplation, and spiritual work for their highest esteem. Thomas Aquinas in *Summa Theologica* affirmed this order: Man's highest act was to know the truth of God in contemplation. Below this was intellectual activity such as copying manuscripts—cleric. Lay brothers who engaged in secular activity were useful and necessary, but the true end of life was to be free from toil.

The men who went out into the world to explore it and to learn its laws were the alchemists, astrologers, and artisans. They became the leaders of the Renaissance—artists, craftsmen, explorers, architects, and scientists. Their work required them to touch materials—stone, sand, plants, and animals. They started a new movement. Work was good for the spirit of man, an idea that arose not from *theory* but from *practice*. As they began to change the face of the earth by fashioning stones into statues and cathedrals, they concluded that work was morally and spiritually good for man.[5]

The Reformation and the industrial revolution that followed brought forth another view of work which challenged the church. Reflecting on this development in the eighteenth century, Adam Smith advanced the thesis in *The Wealth of Nations* that the activity of man is productive when it takes raw material and makes it into something useful. It creates real wealth. Only workers who were fabricators were producers. Smith saw the rise of power machinery, men working by the clock. This was the new order of things. So the ideals of contemplation and work were completely reversed. Only through work measured by the machine and the clock could man really know the worth of life.

Martin Luther looked upon labor as being contrary to nature. God in his providence had given to man all that was needed to sustain life. The idea that work was essential to develop these resources did not seem important to him. Labor was in the world for an educational purpose, training man who had been corrupted by sin; therefore, all work belonged to the realm of natural law, not grace, and was urged upon the common man as a discipline for his spirit.

John Calvin had as his primary aim the establishment of a holy community; therefore, he looked upon work as a calling which should help to order and purify the whole community. He had an ascetic attitude toward work. Hard work was an ideal; laziness was a vice and hurtful to the soul. Through hard work in the secular world, persons could actually begin to establish their holy community even in the secular realm. This community enforced strict laws against luxury but supported a money economy built on trade rather than the agrarian form of society.[6]

The Puritan movement picked upon the Calvinistic ethic and

---

[5] Cf. S. de Grazia, *Of Time, Work and Leisure*, p. 27.
[6] Cf. Ernst Troeltsch, *The Social Teaching of the Christian Churches*, II, 641-50.

gave it a real push in America. Sociologist Robert Merton asserts that the Puritan ethic produced exactly the kind of man needed for the precision, the scientific, and the industrial development of the time. John Wesley operated on the basis of earn all you can (through hard work), save all you can, give all you can. These virtues actually were the base for the economic betterment of the masses in England. By spurring them to untiring industry, cleanliness of habits, prudence in business, temperance, thrift, honesty, and self-reliance, many of them climbed up the social scale to positions of management and business, such as shop-keepers.

In early America the Puritan ethic with its condemnation of leisure as parasitism and work as virtue became the rule of our life. Certain groups in the ante-bellum South pursued the Greek notion that work was a badge of dishonor while it was the duty of the elite to cultivate the mind and the social graces. However, the myths about Paul Bunyan in the West, Mike Fink along the Ohio and Mississippi Rivers, Casey Jones and the railroad, were building the image of work as the means of conquering the wilderness. With the rise of craftsmen, the situation changed somewhat. Workmen obtained real satisfaction out of their fine products. Tool makers, inventors, carpenters, craftsmen highly valued good workmanship.

As technology in the factory system increased and made the contributions of workmen to a product much more complex, value became more obscure. With the rise of managers, bosses, white-collar workers, accountants, personnel directors, salesmen, distributors, work became divorced from the product. As automation controls production, man becomes more of a spectator in the process and is pushed by propaganda to become a compulsive spender in order to keep the wheels of the machine running. The craftsman can find little support for a product in which he has exercised great skill. This is a blow to his integrity. In fact, the consumer is now more important than the producer.

With time on his hands, man feels bored and guilty. In affluent America there is need to reassess our values so that we may accept a high standard of living, utilize our resources better to aid people in their development, cope with our advancing technology, and learn to become free to create a culture that gives meaning to life. If we are to transform free time into leisure, we need to reeducate adults to accept a balance of work and leisure without guilt. Leisure is a life free from work-driven compulsions. Leisure is for renewal, for learning, for freedom, for inquiry, for the rediscovery of meaning and values. Leisure is the relaxed time for reflection. It is freedom from the clock to live in God's time wherein a person may gain a sense of restoration and fulfillment in life.

Toward a Work—Leisure Balance

If work makes the strong man, leisure develops the whole man. Unlike play which is the spontaneous outpouring of activity, leisure is the utilization of time for the inner development of man in reading, thinking, enjoying beauty, and making things. It is time utilized for the cultivation of interpersonal relationships. It is time spent with the cultivation of the arts as a person finds significance in painting, drama, writing, or music. These are intrinsically rewarding, not work for compensation. It is the action of a free man in those causes that better the way of life for mankind. It is a time for growing in the moral and spiritual dimensions of life wherein we contemplate right choices and seek renewal of the inner competence that enables us to live as authentic human beings. Religion has always been at the center of man's leisure activity.

Toward an Authentic Existence

The psychologist Abraham Maslow contends that healthy people who have "gratified the basic needs for safety, belongingness, love, respect and self-esteem" can find a higher sense of fulfillment in "actualization of potentials," fulfillment of mission or calling, and a fuller knowledge and acceptance of their own intrinsic nature.[7] If this is true, millions of people in the United States should be ready to seek a higher form of existence than the accumulation of gadgets as the chief end of being. Can we find a way of life that will enable human beings to find a sense of fulfillment? Can we find meaning in our existence? Is there a way of "being in the world" that gives meaning and authenticity to our existence? Here is the new challenge to Christian laymen today. Can they live in the world and show forth an authentic existence? Can they demonstrate that they have found the clue to freedom in and through Christ so that they do not live like victims overcome by the pressures of our time? Can they witness to the meaning of existence in and through the new quality of wholesomeness they have found in the Christian community?

The German philosopher Martin Heidegger asserts that "authentic existence . . . is respectful of things, respectful of meanings created by past generations as expression of correct possibilities of those epochs, while remaining conscious of its own responsibility as creator of new meaning in casting original light on things-that-are." [8] It was the profound insight of Heidegger that persons find this quality of authenticity (1) in relating the self to reality in the world, (2) in understanding of one's self in relation to others (this involves a quality of really "being there" with persons in sorrow or joy), and (3) in discourse or dialogue that reveals a person's genuine concern. His signs of inauthenticity or phony existence are (1) ambiguity in relation to reality, (2) curiosity that merely examines and never gets involved or never understands, and (3) prattle that says nothing and blocks communication. As one becomes aware of the temporality of life, the end of existence in death, he comes to realize that every

---

[7] *Toward a Psychology of Being*, p. 23.
[8] Cf. T. Langan, *The Meaning of Heidegger*, pp. 23-24.

choice he makes either brings something into the reality of human existence or consigns it to nothingness. This realization enables him to seek a life of care and concern.

Drawing upon the interpretations of Heidegger, the theologian Paul Tillich defines existence as a "standing out" or bringing out of nothingness. We all have potentialities but they are nothing unless we make the choices and the plans to realize them. We realize them in part. Hence the symbol of the fall of man stands as a clue to the meaning of existence. We do not have to be overcome with guilt because of this condition. We can realize our potentialities in part and we can accept our limitations. To be sure, man is free to inquire, to cut himself off from his fellowmen and God or to communicate with both, to create tools, to symbolize, but his freedom is finite. When used as absolute freedom, this leads to estrangement from God and man; when not used, it leads to loss of self and disintegration at the core of one's being. Recognizing this plight, Tillich summons man to have "the courage to be" by accepting the fact that God accepts him in this condition and that Christ has come to reconcile him out of his estrangement from God and his alienation from his fellowmen. In adventuring in this faith, mankind can find a new authenticity for existence amid the ambiguities and pressures of life.[9]

If laymen who have a deep concern for an authentic existence can follow the guidelines of these outstanding thinkers, they can find meaning for their lives. In times past, when Christians were under the duress of persecutors like the Emperor Julian, they were resourceful enough to make their witness and continue the instruction of their children. In times of freedom after the Reformation, they devised laws, composed music, wrote books, and created art forms that symbolized and enriched the new

[9] Cf. Paul Tillich, *Systematic Theology*, II, 29-33.

culture. (See chapter 2.) They were makers of history. We can enter into the heritage of both groups. Today laymen are challenged to rise above the status of victims of machine technology, to accept the new freedom that technology can offer, to bring its developments into their service so that they may be free to find the fullness of existence as human beings.

Reeducation for a New Style of Life

In Chicago a large department store has employed fifty defiant young adults. Three days a week they work in the store in good surroundings. Three days a week they study in a special school. Through the use of counseling, controlled group relations, and apprentice training they are fashioning a new style of life. This balance between work and the wise use of leisure is helping them develop a more wholesome perspective of life. Why? The Christian personnel manager who looks upon his vocation as a challenge gave this reply. "Someday they may be able to hear the word 'redemption' and respond to it with integrity because it happened to them." Perhaps this incident can give us a clue to a new approach to witness to the authenticity of our Christian faith. Through work and leisure people can develop a new style of living that overcomes compulsive labor, boredom, oppressive routinization, and violence as a way of escape from the victimization of environment. Young people who get launched into the world of work so they may be responsible participants in creating the service needed for life gain a sense of integrity, can accept themselves and find fulfillment for the potential within them.

Each year a half million executives return to colleges and universities to study liberal arts. They take courses in ethics, philosophy, art, music, literature, etc. Why? As one corporation vice-president put it, "I'm tired of having men around me who know all the technical answers to the problems we face, but don't know any of the real questions to ask about life." Leisure is meant for learning. These men are probing the great questions and the glorious heritage of meaning found by persons in the past so that the time of their lives may be enriched with the moral, spiritual, and aesthetic values that have given dignity to man's being and purpose to his existence. Technology is a means to making a living. It takes a whole being to live authentically.

As the years of existence are extended and retirement comes at an earlier age, we must seek to release the experience, wisdom, and skill of aging persons for the enrichment of mankind. Too many of them have their talents wrapped in mummy cloth today. Early retirement cuts adults off from life, puts them on the shelf, consigns them to the back room. They need to be retrained for senior churchmanship as well as senior citizenship. Older adults are finding meaning for their lives as they help school dropouts improve their reading skills and learn to participate in the class room. Older adults are being retrained as visitors to homebound and hospitalized persons so that they may fulfill their ministry to their fellowmen. Older adults gain a sense of responsibility as they participate in church and community forums on health and medical care, investments, housing arrangements, and world affairs. They are consultants, advisors, volunteers. They write the history of the church and the community. They set up and staff church libraries so that reading rooms may be open to persons throughout the week. They engage in study and discussion groups, attend lectures, concerts, and dramas. They read and discuss good books. In fact, it is now possible for most older persons to learn as long as they live and to make a significant contribution to life for a much greater period of time. With the plan for retirement from work each person needs to explore the opportunities in leisure for significant participation in our time.

CONCLUSIONS

Each individual is an event in time. He is a history, a being and a becoming. It is up to everyone to claim the present moment

as that opportunity in time when the creative pontential within
him may be summoned for partial realization of the contribution
which he will make for the future of mankind.

Chapter 8
Bibliography

Buckingham, W. *Automation*. New York: Mentor, New American
Library, 1963.

Come, A. *Agents of Reconciliation*. Philadelphia: Westminster Press,
1960.

Cox, Harvey. *The Secular City*. New York: Macmillan, 1965.

Cumming, Elaine and Henry, William E. *Growing Old*. New York:
Basic Books, 1961.

de Grazia, S. *Of Time, Work, and Leisure*. Garden City, N .Y.:
Doubleday-Anchor, 1964.

Donahue, Wilma and others, eds. *Free Time: Challenge to Later
Maturity*. Ann Arbor: University of Michigan Press, 1958.

Gray, Robert M. and Moberg, David O. *Church and the Older
Person*. Grand Rapids: Eerdmans, 1962.

Langen, T. *The Meaning of Heidegger*. New York: Columbia Press,
1959.

Lee, R. *Religion and Leisure in America*. New York: Abingdon
Press, 1964.

Maslow, A. H. *Toward a Psychology of Being*. Princeton: Van
Nostrand, 1962.

Nash, J. *Philosophy of Recreation and Leisure*. Dubuque: W. C.
Brown, 1960.

Robinson, J. A. T. *On Being the Church in the World*. Philadelphia:
Westminster Press, 1960.

————. *Honest to God*. Philadelphia: Westminster Press, 1963.

Tillich, P. *Systematic Theology, Vol. II*. Chicago: University of Chicago Press, 1957.

Troeltsch, E. *The Social Teaching of the Christian Churches*. New York: Macmillan, 1959.

Trueblood, Elton. *Your Other Vocation*. New York: Harper, 1952.

Wiener, Norbert. *The Human Use of Human Beings: Cybernetics and Society*. New York: Doubleday, 1954.

Winter, G. *The New Creation as Metropolis*. New York: Macmillan, 1963.

_____. "Recreation in the Age of Automation," Annals of American Academy of Political and Social Science. Philadelphia, Pa., Sept. 1957.

Chapter 9

Family Life—Christian Style

Cultural pluralism challenges Christian families to create new forms of ministry and nurture in the Christian faith and style of life. No longer can parents assume that their children will get a coherent system of beliefs from the communities they inhabit. Suburbia, small town, and inner city are becoming pluralistic. Many sects, cults, and religious groups compete vigorously for the loyalties of every person. They support conflicting beliefs and value systems. Also, parents who expect to have specialists at church, people who teach dancing and music or instruct their children in religion, will find themselves caught in time traps and chauffeuring chores that disrupt and block consistent learning sequences. Public schools are the focal point of so many pressure groups that at best they have become purveyors of generalized schemes of democratic values without the interpretation of the meanings of faith that support them. In the midst of this cultural milieu the family is called to be the center for the formation and interpretation of a Christian style of life that can engage in creative encounter with other cultural patterns in the community.

Can the Family Become a Center of Cultural Change?

Can the family fulfill these expectations? Many critics answer, "No." They contend that the family is trapped by mass media —television, radio, newspapers and magazines—to the extent that it cannot rise above reporters and observers to develop a Christian critique of culture. Contemporary man is so imbued with the television image of man that he does not want it otherwise. He likes to be a pleasure-loving consumer whose chief end in life is to buy gadgets and enjoy entertainment forever. He will not respond to the biblical insight, that he is made in the image of God. Man is so pleasure-loving, gadget-oriented that he cannot rise above this cultural trap and examine himself in relation to the television hero. All this is a form of cultural determinism that Christians cannot accept.

If the Christian family is going to extricate itself from this kind of social trap, it must take seriously some of the new responsibilities which it confronts and become aware of the kinds of experiences in which some new learnings can take place. Today the family is called upon to clarify the male and female roles in life so that young men and young women may gain a sense of their true identity and find a true fulfillment in their relationships with one another. Members must make a more conscious effort to support long-term goals that lead to the ultimate fulfillment of life in preference to passing satisfactions. The family must deliberately choose to live by love-inspired relationships that develop attitudes of respect for others as persons. In such a family sacrifices will need to be made so that others may find fulfillment. Distorted images of other people, groups, and of oneself need to be clarified. Sex is to be interpreted in terms of freedom and responsibility wherein the rights of others are respected. In the family persons will need to find deliverance from the forces that dehumanize life. Amid pressures Christian families must assert their freedom to live as persons and develop a style of life that enables them to grow into fullness of maturity as moral, rational, social, and spiritual beings. From this kind of base Christians can move into society renewed in spirit and strengthened to be persons of integrity in the world.

CONFORMITY VERSUS FREEDOM

Some critics contend that families are so enamored of middle-class values, captivated by the cult of conformity, that they can never become free enough to deviate from it. It is granted readily that the conditions of life in our ideology-ridden and highly pressured existence trap us day after day. Recognition that we are trapped in a lot of mediocre routines that do not give life much significance is a degree of freedom. When we realize that we have been caught with our insecurity showing because we foolishly bought something out of compulsion, we can begin to search for values that are more enduring. When we realize that inner security and integrity is something which we cannot buy, then we can begin to change by being "transformed in spirit."

The Christian family is never completely captive in any culture because it puts its faith in God's new age that is always coming into man's existence. This faith saves him from becoming completely captivated by the idolatries of our passing culture. As families in America change their style of life from that of an agricultural and small-town society to an urbanized one, this Christian perspective can save members of families from nostalgic attachment to obsolete values that are passing away and from uncritical acceptance of an emerging, impersonalized urbanity that may be a new form of idolatry. Any family that seeks to influence a Christian style of life will need to develop a God-related perspective that enables it to cope with change and the everrising claims of new idolatries.

Contemporary culture includes a rising and insistent demand for new personal liberties. This is articulated in the college halls in demonstrations for free speech. It appears in many forms as protest against the current sex ethics which have controlled personal behavior through external restraints. Young people are clamoring for the rights of individual decisions in their intimate personal relationships. This new challenge to young people places new responsibilities upon every family to help them grow to maturity in ways that will guide them in the inner workings of beliefs and values that determine choices toward a worthwhile style of life. Today's American girl is confronted by a Miss Boardwalk, a cultural model with whom she must identify, who epitomizes all the consumer values of society and dispenses her charms on perfumes and cosmetics. In spiked heels and swimsuit, this modern Aphrodite projects an image of calibrated femininity upon all her lonely followers. The values she represents are fleeting—success, creature comforts, popularity. Upon the millions of her followers who must live with a sense of alienation, routinized work, and a feeling of rejection, she not only forces an impossible image but impresses the longing for unrealizable satisfactions. In frustration and quiet despair, the vast majority of persons must work out in an entirely different context their true identity and find expression for the feelings of intimacy that are a part of being human. Asserting one's freedom to be oneself amid these pressures calls for family support.

If the relationship between men and God is going to be vital, members of the family will need to be conscious of it and cultivate it amid the pressures of propaganda. In industry a person trusts a machine when he knows it will operate in exactly the same way under rigid controls. In the family we trust persons because they will act with freedom in accordance with their own beliefs and values. They may or may not act in the same way continuously. It is a matter of rejoicing when their powers of discerning alternatives expand and their abilities to cope with an increasing number of complex situations enlarge. When persons are being taken in by the many idols of our culture, they need to be related to one another with a filial bond of trust so that they may strengthen one another's relation to God. This relationship to God can never allow them to settle for a pleasure-seeking, gadget-buying state of alienation from their true selves or for a mad race to be like their neighbors because of a low sense of personal worth. This is the dimension of faith that must be cultivated in the family so that we may live as free persons who have a true self-image and who can negotiate with trust their relationships with others in the world.

Eric Erikson has pointed out that this sense of identity, of discovering who you really are, is the most important discovery of adolescence. The whole coterie of leaders in education who were brought up on the school of "adjustment" psychology do not help much. "The point is not that the student learns to sell himself or that he abandons his integrity but that he is discouraged from using his own sense of himself," declares E. Z. Friedenberg. "He gets no help in learning to turn to himself for support in times of adversity or for inner discipline in times of seductive prosperity." [1] Amid all the pressures—social, intellectual, work-orientation, religious pluralism, play, governmental, army, etc.—the Christian family remains the crucible in which one's images are tested, clarified, and brought together into a continuing style of living that gives meaning to one's existence.

[1] *The Vanishing Adolescent,* p. 109.

ALIENATION TO COMMUNICATION

The process of wholesome self-realization within the family is the product of more than meeting one's own personal needs, Maslow points out that self-actualization leads beyond tension reduction to vocation and a sense of mission.[2] Self-actualizing people are not dependent for their development upon what mother, cousin, or some father figure says to them in praise or blame. They depend upon their own resources to face the crises and hardships of life. This requires the need for an inner competence which cannot always be relied upon. If there is deficiency in one's inner need fulfillment or if too much anxiety is aroused through external pressures, a person will tend to distort what he hears to satisfy these needs. The continuous expression of need fulfillment may lead to overdependency upon others in the family to supply love, feelings of belonging, or esteem.[3] Such overdependency is unhealthy and may lead to withdrawal from activities and encounters in life. Such people view the church as a hide-out shelter into which a person retreats from the storms of life. Or overdependency may lead to a deep sense of alienation in which a person exhibits periods of rebellion, tension, and fear. Such retreats into escapist piety or overzealous activism are symptoms of an unhealthy religion.

The fact that we are language- and thought-using persons indicates that we are intended for communication. "This intentionalism gives rise to two fundamental categories of thought: the explicatory function and the implicatory function," contends Jean Piaget. In the former, "the mind turns to the external world," in the latter, "the mind turns inward to analysis of intentions and of their relation."[4] Communication involves turning the mind outward and listening to the other person; it implies also appropriating meaning from this experience and in-

[2] Cf. M. Jahoda, *Current Concepts of Mental Health*, pp. 33, 47.
[3] Cf. H. S. Sullivan, *The Interpersonal Theory of Psychiatry*, chap. 10.
[4] *The Language and Thought of the Child*, p. 236.

ternalizing it. If the mind of the child or the adult is completely absorbed in its own needs, hurts, or anxieties, he will hear only those symbols that refer to his needs. Real communication implies a balance between listening with understanding to what goes on inside the mind of the other person, internalizing what has been said so that it may be related to what one really is, and then speaking out of one's own integrity in dialogue with the other person.

This process is aided when the home is a forum of faith in which affirmation and doubt can be expressed in freedom. No one is grading you. Each is eager that you learn to express the beliefs that are genuinely you. Articulation of these beliefs is facilitated when parents realize that the search for identity is a lifelong concern for all members of the family, not adolescents alone. Even mother who takes in stride the jobs of chauffeur, house manager, treasurer, cook, club chairman, nurse, etc., develops qualities of self-reliance so that she may keep these activities in perspective as she reflects with maturity upon their significance for that continuity of meanings that make up her own true identity. Mother too, asks the question: Who am I? Her answer is more complex. The minds of children, youth, and adults can bridge the span of the years when each speaks out of the persistent concerns which he is truly seeking to absorb. If adults accept this psychological fact, they may overcome many of the breakdowns in communication which separate them from children today. Through this process each may discover who he is, what he believes, and gain support in his efforts to communicate with integrity the truth which he embodies.

The Christian family is the arena of faith in which this art of dialogue encourages a person to speak with intimacy and openness so that true communication as a child of God with other persons who accept him as he really is makes possible the act of revelation (which is self-disclosure) and reconciliation (which is acceptance and forgiveness). In this community of faith and doubt, persons can drop the protective mask of pretense or threat and search for those relationships wherein one's authentic being can meet with what is genuine in the other person. Within the context of the Christian family, persons may be renewed in spirit, saved from the blight of alienation that plagues us daily, and restored to a communicative relationship with others. This process enables us to face in continuity the encounters with the world with resilience and wholesomeness, and members of the family may thereby prepare themselves to influence the culture of their community with Christian beliefs.

FINDING MEANING FOR EXISTENCE

Formerly a primary role of a father was the preparation of his son for work in the world. On the farm he taught him the basic skills of agriculture; in the home workshop, the use of tools for industry. In a world where the sons and daughters must move into an economy which changes its methods of production continuously, a new kind of orientation is necessary. If the machine is going to be driven by the machine, who is going to ask the computer the right questions, and who will feed in the right data? This fact puts a new responsibility upon fathers. Can they keep alive the curiosity, the spirit of inquiry in the lives of their sons so that they may be able to make the breakthroughs necessary for survival? Moreover, can they interpret this universe from a theistic perspective that is built upon contemporary understandings of reality?

Today our homes can become cultural centers. Great books produced in paperbacks may be purchased for nominal sums. Radio and television may keep a continuous flow of information streaming into our households. Everywhere around us ideas, opinions, and images abound. From this spinning nebula of impressions, how may we bring into being structures of knowledge that give meaning to our lives? In his novels Albert Camus exclaims that life is absurd, irrational, and meaningless.[5]

Franz Kafka in his novel, *The Trial*, has used symbolic language to depict a very important truth for our time. By the use of double meanings for "arrested" (taken into custody/stopped in development), he portrays powerfully the plight of modern man. The plot reveals that the protagonist, although taken by the police from his bed, was really arrested in his development, namely through an empty, routinized, bored, nonproductive existence. In commenting upon this novel, Erich Fromm points to the fact that all his life the hero was striving to receive from others, never to give. The strangest part of this dreamlike existence is that the hero can go through all the experiences of life "arrested." [6] As the plot continues, it becomes more evident that the hero is unable to relate himself to men. Whenever he confronts a man in authority, he submits completely, or rebels, or runs away. He never learns how to cope with authority, to test his experiences against it, to absorb them and appropriate meanings from them, and to believe enough in himself to venture in faith on his own. Being unable to develop this amount of self-understanding and self-discipline, he cannot understand what his conscience is saying, so he thrusts himself upon external authorities—lawyer, judge, inspector, priest—who, because they must speak as authority figures, weaken him further. His dream ends in a nightmare of destruction. However, in facing death, he perceives the sterility of his life and summons enough faith to begin inquiring about its meaning.

With deep insight Kafka points to the need for persons to per-

---

[5] In *The Myth of Sisyphus and Other Essays*, Albert Camus likens life to a man rolling a huge boulder uphill. It is so overwhelming that he is crushed by it.

In *The Plague*, he describes certain moral actions in a crisis, but in the end all are caught in the irrational forces of good and evil.

In *The Rebel*, he calls man to revolt against his tragic plight that makes him victim of nature and creation.

[6] *The Forgotten Language*, pp. 249-63.

ceive clearly the father and mother roles in the family. Symbolically, the role of father is interpreter of moral values, he is disciplinarian and instrumentalist. He teaches the children how to handle authority. To cope with its demands, one must match its strength, wrestle with it, come to grips with it, negotiate with it. Children who have been denied this kind of experience in the home will have to find ways of compensating for it elsewhere or become arrested in their development. The style of life which the child develops in relation to necessity, moral demands, and authority structures tends to persist throughout life. If a person learns early to react to obstacles by running away, he will tend to continue doing it and never really learn to cope with life. If a person tends to become submissive each time he confronts an authority figure, he will tend to develop a dependency-rebellion relationship to external pressure, in which he may never internalize their meanings as his own. If a person begins to believe that he is essentially good so that he can take criticism, weigh it, appropriate its meaning for himself, he is developing a style of life that has meaning for himself, allows for flexibility in participation and continuity in development.

Likewise the role of motherhood in our culture is related to permissiveness, supportiveness, provider of food and love. Our culture expects a daughter to learn these roles from her mother. The way in which a mother seeks to impart her understanding of these roles may vary widely depending upon the temperament and needs of the child. When this kind of love relationship is denied or distorted, the child may develop a very low sense of esteem toward himself.[7] Feeling worthless or ashamed the child may become especially sensitive to other persons. If they respond with acceptance, the child may be drawn to the group for the fulfillment of this affection need. For the child, the gang may mean that they are a generalized mother substitute.

[7] Cf. T. Parsons and R. F. Bales *Family: Socialization and Interaction Process*, pp. 160-78.

In the majority of families today two factors are at work that completely disrupt the traditional roles of father and mother. They are absenteeism of father and the work-oriented relationships of mother. If father leaves town Monday and returns Friday, mother can hardly postpone all discipline problems until Saturday night. There would be little or no connection in experience between the discipline and the deed. If limits of behavior are to be set, they should be set in relation to the activity, not in relation to some other activity at another time. Postponement may set up the wrong relationship of deed and discipline so that confusion reigns and a child never learns self-discipline. Each day that mother works, she enters into the world of competition and strife. These involvements affect the whole way of life. If mother brings home her competitive style of life and relates to the members of the family as a competitor instead of the one who furnishes the supporting love relationships, confusion and frustration will abound. If a child comes to mother seeking love and support, only to be manipulated by mother to get something done, we are going to have a lot more angry young men and women on our hands because they have been arrested in their love-supporting and love-encouraging development.

The family is a center for learning self-identity and the negotiation of relationships (person-to-person communication). Through role identification persons learn who they are as human beings as well as the instrumental skills for getting things done in our society. Through the negotiation of interpersonal relationships the child learns ways of belonging, feelings of acceptance that are so essential for changing, as a person negotiates his relationships with others in the world. When role confusion abounds, parents must find new ways of enabling all members of the family to negotiate these tasks, so that they may develop the self-images and skills in relationships that will give real meaning to life.

The Christian style of life in the family encourages each member to take some initiative in the search for the meaning of life. Amid the deluge of facts that inundate schooling which puts a premium on quantities of right answers and work routines, the family as the church has an educational ministry. Within it, members can ask one another some of the important questions about life: Why are we here? What is the meaning of my life? What is the real destiny of man? What does it mean to be a human being? What understandings of God make sense to us? What helps me change so that I may cope with my existence? How do I make responsible decisions in our culture? What aspects of Christian discipleship give the most satisfaction in life? Some of the great dramatists, novelists, poets of our time raise the issues that need to be faced in our families. It is up to us to discuss them in the home, to bring the Christian perspective to bear upon them and thereby include all ages in a meaningful search for existence. Harvard educator Jerome S. Bruner indicates that life's great questions can be faced honestly by children at any age. The phrasing may need to be correlated with the vocabulary of the person, but the persistent search for meaning continues throughout life.[8] This search is as integral to the Christian style of life as birth, growth, and death itself.

It is the measured judgment of Gordon Allport of Harvard that a person's cognitive style of life tends to be related to the patterns of thinking in the family. "A person who is insecure, self-distrustful, who feels threatened by life or otherwise inadequate, tends to have a cognitive style which is rigid, field-bound, concrete, acquiescent," concludes Allport. "By contrast, the more active, able, secure, relaxed individual is able to perceive and think in channels that are flexible and, on the whole,

* Cf. *The Process of Education*, pp. 33-54.

better adapted to the objective demands of the situation he finds himself in." [9] These basic perceptions filter the knowledge a person accepts and tend to organize it into a belief and value system.

It is here in the midst of life the family that persons fulfill their roles as the "priesthood of believers." As they engage in discourse with others, asking questions, clarifying relationships, listening and responding with understanding and graciousness, they are performing acts of ministry to other persons. As they enable members to reconcile differences, thereby restoring relationships between them, they are making manifest the reconciling work of God in the world. As they help others attain fulfillment in the realization of goals, they are being servants of God in the world. If Christian parents of children under the persecution of Julian were able to continue the teaching ministry of the church in their homes with adaptiveness, parents today amid our knowledge revolution should be able to help young people become intelligently oriented to our world with a faith that reflects ultimate reality with accuracy and integrity.

TOWARD MATURITY IN LOVE

Above all, the style of life in the Christian family affords its members the opportunity to grow toward maturity in love. It provides the climate wherein expressions of intimacy and affection are given and received. Through these expressions the small child learns to feel secure and gains a sense of being wanted. He becomes sensitive to the needs of others and explores ways of relating himself to them. This leads to the expanding of interests in and appreciation of others. When experiences of hurt and hate are encountered, the family becomes a source of restitution and recovery. When a child becomes dis-

* *Pattern and Growth in Personality*, p. 270.

pleased with life and reacts with hostility, the family can lead
him to truer perceptions of reality and still relate to him with
warmth and support.

Love adds zest, spontaneity and a quality of depth to all relationships in the family. It can help to set the adolescent free to
explore the wonderful world of persons. It enables him to overcome selfishness and to be outgoing toward others. It empowers
the adolescent to move toward independence, friendship, court-
ship, and later marriage. It enables couples to consider many aspects of their relationships—physical, emotional, economic, educational, social, religious, ideational, and to make choices in
which they can find fulfillment of life together. In Christian
perspective, marriage is a sacred-covenant relationship based
upon fidelity in love. In the Gospel of Mark, Jesus places marriage in the context of continuing creation and providence of
God, not on the basis of Mosaic law. (See Mark 10.) In this
perspective it opens dimensions of grace and spiritual depths
which bring some of the deepest satisfactions of life. Likewise the
privileges and responsibilities of parenthood are seen as more
than biological processes. They are viewed as cooperation with
God in the process of bringing new life into the world and of
nurturing it to purposeful maturity.

Unfortunately there are many forces in our sensate culture
that seek to oversell sex. The merchants of bottled and costumed
femininity have succeeded in selling a tremendous number of
teen-agers on the notion that the chief end of women is biological.
Likewise psychiatrists who peddle the doctrine of "escape from
frustration," as well as the movie heroines who always get their
man, compound the "feminine mystique." In her angry disclaim-
er, Betty Friedan contends that such a pitch has succeeded in
burying millions of women alive. "If women do not put forth
that effort to become all that they have it in them to become,
they will forfeit their humanity," she exclaims. "A woman today
who has no goal, no purpose, no ambition patterning her days

into the future, making her stretch and grow beyond that small score of years in which her body can fill its biological function, is committing a kind of suicide." [10] Harsh words? Overstated? Perhaps, but they signal a turning point in the thinking of thousands who fled into marriage as an escape from the challenge of our complex living only to find they were thwarted in their true development. When persons awaken to their victimization by a sensate culture, they may be freed to explore a way of life that places sex in the larger context of love wherein responsible participation leads to wholesomeness and mutual well-being.

The Christian family brings a redeeming influence to bear upon the sensate view of love. It views the life of love in the perspective of what God has done for mankind. It supports persons in their efforts to be considerate and helpful of others. It respects the autonomy of the other person, yet instills a genuine sense of compassion and willingness to serve or sacrifice for others. It encourages a sense of appreciation of other people. Love is given freely and spontaneously because of the family's trust in and reliance upon God.

CONCLUSION

As families seek to embody the Christian style of life, they will encounter many families with a different style of life. Some of them are tradition bound so that they make all decisions upon the basis of what may have been customary in the community. The Christian family can confront them with a new freedom that enables them to rise above the boredom of routinization while finding an inner discipline that can steer between too much liberty leading to despair and too much conformity leading to self-destruction.

To the family which asserts that it can "buy everything," the Christian style of family life reveals inner spiritual values

[10] *The Feminine Mystique*, pp. 324-25.

that save the Christian from being trapped by sensuousness or guilt and thinking that the accumulation of "things that are solid" can bring real security to life.

To the family that believes that the chief end of man is to "do as one pleases," the Christian family presents a community which enables the individual with deep feelings of alienation to find restoration of relationships and communication facilitated because of persons who can listen deeply with understanding and enable members to speak with integrity. The Christian style saves the "do-as-you-please individualist" from an alienation that destroys him.

To those families being pushed into insensitivity by the mechanization and urbanization factors in our culture, the Christian style of family life offers a chance to grow toward maturity in love that overcomes distrust on the one hand and being victimized by sensuousness on the other. Through the intimate relationships expressed in the family, persons live as if their lives and the lives of others were a trust from God. From this perspective, persons find grace to accept others in moments of joy and trial and to respect others as persons of worth. It enables parents to check the impulse of squeezing children into their preconceived molds. Christian love enables people to sacrifice, to serve unselfishly, and to support others in their efforts to become what God intends them to be.

Chapter 9
Bibliography

Allport, G. W. *Pattern and Growth in Personality*. New York: Holt, Rinehart, & Winston, 1961.

Bruner, Jerome S. *The Process of Education*. Cambridge: Harvard University Press, 1960.

Camus, Albert. *The Myth of Sisyphus and Other Essays.* New York: Vintage, 1955.

——. *The Plague.* New York: Knopf, 1948.

——. *The Rebel.* New York: Knopf, 1954.

Dunbar, Flanders. *Your Preteenager's Mind and Body.* New York: Hawthorn, 1962.

Duvall, Evelyn M. *Family Development.* Philadelphia: Lippincott, 1962.

Egleson, Jim and Janet. *Parents Without Partners.* New York: Act books, 1961.

Fairchild, Roy W. and John C. Wynn, *Families in the Church.* New York: Association Press, 1961.

Friedan, B. *The Feminine Mystique.* New York: Dell, 1963.

Friedenberg, Edgar Z. *The Vanishing Adolescent.* Boston: Beacon Press, 1959.

Fromm, E. *The Forgotten Language.* New York: Grove Press, 1957.

Howe, Reuel L. *Herein Is Love.* Valley Forge: Judson, 1961.

Hymes, James L., Jr. *Understanding Your Child.* Englewood Cliffs: Prentice-Hall, 1952.

Jahoda, M. *Current Concepts of Mental Health.* New York: Basic Books, Inc., 1958.

Mace, David R. *Success in Marriage.* Nashville: Abingdon Press, 1958.

Miller, Randolph C. *Christian Insights for Marriage.* Nashville: Abingdon Press, 1961.

Parsons, T. and Bales, R. F. *Family: Socialization and Interaction Process.* Glencoe: Free Press, 1955.

Piaget, J. *The Language and Thought of the Child.* New York: Meridian, 1955.

Stirling, Nora. *Family Life Plays.* Nashville: Abingdon Press, 1961.

Sullivan, H. S. *The Interpersonal Theory of Psychiatry.* New York: Norton, 1953.

Whyte, Dorothy K. *Teaching Your Child Right from Wrong.* New York: Bobbs-Merrill, 1961.

Chapter 10

God's New Age

Mankind stands at an exit and in an entrance. The past is truly a prologue from which he learns much about the present. Yet his story is coming into being moment by moment. Arnold Toynbee points out that life can become so adapted and adjusted to forms of the past that there is little energy remaining to change in accordance with the requirements of the future.[1] Contemplating the future is not without its nemesis either. It lies in idolization—the creation of a society that obscures the tragic, the evil that is in human history. Man is a history-making being. Out of his freedom to choose and build for the future

[1] Cf. A Study of History, I, 327.

arise the mistakes, the wrong choices that prove fatal to coviliza-
tion after civilization.

THE AGE WE ARE ENTERING

The age into which we are now moving may be characterized
by rapid scientific advances which outrun the social and political
structures that utilize them. Atomic power has placed in the
hands of leaders the power to destroy mankind. Atomic radiation
creates mutations that may have far-reaching implications for
life in the future. Can man control these mutations? Communications satellites make the world an international vista vision
onto which an incident in a remote corner of Africa or Asia is
broadcast in an instant throughout all nations. Space travel has
been enhanced by new forms of thrust so that interplanetary
contact and exporation may confront us with entirely new species
and forms of life. Automation is carrying the industrial revolution into a new phase wherein machines run machines so that
masses of mankind must find new forms of work. More and
more life is concentrated in huge urban complexes which increase mobility, anxiety, and the impersonalization of life. More
new nations have arisen in the last decade than at any time
since the Reformation.

Will man's tendency toward idolization cause him to elevate
the new technology to the place of God in the new age? Will he
espouse the utopian faith that science can save us? Will he become so accustomed to the impersonalization of life that the
rituals of mechanized travel, mechanized communication, and
mechanized living anesthetize his relationships and obscure what
it means to be a human being? Will our decisions in the future
be made more and more by computers that devour tons of mathematics and social data, causing values to be considered irrelevant
in the economic, political, and social areas of life? Will the
machines make the fatal mistake of our civilization?

These questions are causing contemporary man to pause in the midst of his activities and to reflect upon the destiny of life. Plagued by the overwhelming desire for expressing himself, driven by the urged for power, and lured by the goals of materialistic success, a young adult sets forth with vigor to "get the most out of life." When he pauses for reflection in the midst of life, he finds himself overwhelmed by feelings of confusion, anxiety, and futility. These feelings are symptoms of a sick soul. His confusion implies that man has made his choices in terms of wrong scales of values; his anxiety implies that he feels a threat to himself at the very moment when he tries to exert power over others; and his futility implies that he has discovered the meaninglessness of the effort he is putting forth in life to realize some false goals. It is apparent that Christians, confronting this situation, are called upon to reassess their way of being in the world to make a worthwhile future possible.

WHAT ALTERNATIVES ARE BEFORE US?

If modern man turns to secular organizations for a remedy to cure this malady, he is confronted with the admonition to accentuate the things he is doing—but to do them with more efficiency. Yet the inner recesses of his own soul cry out for new perceptions of truth, integrity, courage, freedom, and spirit and he knows that his feelings of emptiness persist. If he goes to sources of mass culture—television, radio, movies, novels, or drama—his anxiety is heightened. The one central theme that these media convey with an unceasing din is the theme of Greek tragedy without its heroes. In Greek tragedy man was caught in the web of fate. The best of our modern playwrights rewrite this old theme. Tennessee Williams' *The Glass Menagerie* points out a young lady so caught in the web of oversolicitous mother love that she could never enter into wholesome marriage. In *Death of a Salesman*, Arthur Miller shows Willie Loman caught by the illusion that he could make a million. In *The Crucible* he writes about a heroine caught in the web of community prejudice. In *A Streetcar Named Desire* Tennessee Williams combines the impacts of these mass media which snare man in the futility of trying to escape from the boredom of life by consuming more goods. In the deep recesses of his own soul he yearns for deliverance from evil and some purpose that gives a sense of direction to life.

When modern man tries to save himself in a big organization, he ends up becoming alienated from his own selfhood. In *These Things Remain* Carlyle Marney describes the inner feeling of such a man with devastating accuracy.

You will catch your ride or your bus or fight for a parking place; and another day will be upon you. On your way to town you will develop heartburn from having hurried too much, from having eaten the wrong things too fast; so you will take a Tum to sooth it, with some patented, foaming elixir in a drugstore glass, and then you will open the door to your temple. You will check stock, or sort vegetables, or read yesterday's mail. Soon you will squeeze a pair of shoes onto a customer, or you will look for hat-sizes, or you will weigh turnips . . . . Then it is coffee time, sacred interval, and you get a break. A little bit picked up in spirit, you will come back to work and worry about the children's report cards, your daughter's dating habits or that she either did or will marry the wrong fellow too young, last month's bills, the neighbor's fence line; maybe you ought to see the doctor about yourself, yet "I have worked twenty years and have no savings at all except the little bit of elapsed insurance"—and you are glad to have it and wish the premiums were paid. Then lunch time—blessed break! You swallow a bowl of soup, bolt a sandwich, wonder why you are nervous; some drugstore radio blares the news of one general's important word to another general's word—you wish you knew which set of stars on which shoulder had all the right of it and in the back of your mind you feel a little guilty because you are not more concerned. But the whole business drops through the grating of your mind and out of sight for you must go by and make a payment on that small loan overdue—and to do it you borrow from another small loan outfit until payday.[2]

After such a day, the modern successful man crawls into bed at night saying,

Nothing that I did today matters! If I had put a label on everything that I did today, it would read "This product is not guaranteed beyond sixty days. It wasn't put together right, it wasn't made of the right stuff, it won't stand up under use; it will break down." If I hadn't done a thing all day, it wouldn't matter; nothing I do matters or counts or lasts after payday.[3]

After this brief meditation, he collapses into sleep, knowing in the deep recesses of his soul that the possession of economic goods is not the highest destiny of a moral-spiritual being.

CAN SCIENCE SAVE US?

Overawed by the wonders of science which propel objects in space at fantastic rates of speed, send messages around the world by satellite in an instant, and calculate by computer with incredible swiftness and accuracy, contemporary man turns to science to save him. He listens to the words of physicists as if they were clairvoyant in politics and international relations. Modern man, remembering that Otto Hahn split the nucleus of uranium in 1938, that Albert Einstein described it to President Roosevelt, that Enrico Fermi produced the first chain reaction in Chicago, and that in 1945 the first atomic bomb was dropped upon Hiroshima, expects the manufacturers of the product to point the way to existence in the future. But technology which utilizes quantities of mathematics to unleash new quantities of energy cannot create a future in which man can control the process which may destroy all life upon the earth. Nor can it

[2] Pp. 14, 15.
[3] *Ibid.*, p. 16.

lead men back into some blissful, preatomic Garden of Eden. The knowledge of Hahn, Curie, Einstein, Bohr, and Heisenberg is now a part of our culture and belongs to the facts of life with which we must live through all our future days. The technology which the scientists have produced does not threaten man. Rather he threatens himself. This technology places new demands upon him to change so that he understand his present historical situation and be able to meet the future. Here is the imperative truth of our time—man must change. If we are going to enter God's new age, we must begin to perceive human beings differently, relate to them as moral and spiritual beings, and make those choices that make the future possible. The kind of thinking that produced the computer and the atomic bomb will not point the way to this kind of future.

Secularism, big organization, and science are giant forces at work trying to determine our future. God is at work in many ways, within and outside the churches, providing for the conditions of life. If man is to discover a reason for being, he will have to look beyond the secular, organizational, and scientific sources of knowledge. Boredom, moral nihilism, and the sheer utilization of power for the sake of power could drive modern man to destroy himself in a desperate renunciation of the meaninglessness of life. It is the Christian interpretation of history that opens up the meaning of creation and providence, judgment, reformation, the relationship of God to history in Jesus Christ, and the outcome of history in the plan of God. These interpretations not only provide a reason for being in the world but a way of participating in history that enables persons to make the choices that bring life-sustaining ends into the actuality. Mankind can survive if it can find the ways to bring new forms of order to bear upon the control of new energy forces, new unity among the nations that have come of age, and a new wholesomeness to the relationships between the races of men.

WHAT IS REQUIRED OF CHRISTIANS?

If Christians are going to enter creatively and redemptively into God's newly emerging age, they must do three things. First, they must understand what God is doing now in the world. Only when a Christian can identify himself with his biblical heritage and history as man made in the image of God to have dominion over areas of natural life and to use his power responsibly, can he enter into the creative processes of history today. Secondly, Christians must help the churches recapture the biblical view of destiny which includes the whole range of biblical faith, not one book, one chapter, or one verse of the Bible. Thirdly, Christian laymen must try to master the dynamic factors that set men free to change so that they may enable their fellowmen to overcome the sense of futility concerning their own actions and to participate creatively in God's redemptive processes.

FINDING ONE'S IDENTITY IN HERITAGE

Contemporary man lives on a veritable midway at the county fair. He is surrounded by pitchmen offering some solution to his woes. Each barker has an image of contemporary man which his remedies would fulfill. Some see him as a pleasure-seeking animal who needs fulfillment as a playboy in somewhat opulent surroundings. Others view him as a creature in need of adjustment. Their cry is, "Conform!" However, when one is in the midst of eight or ten revolutions all going on at the same time, conformity may increase inner conflict. Many persons regard man as a customer who is always right if he continues to buy. But the accumulation of more and more goods can cut persons off from neighbors who are envious. Others regard man as a rational being. With more education he might guide history, but a quick review of Dachau, Hiroshima, Lidice brings to mind searing flames that melt the veneer of rationality.

Christian man dares to confront secular man with the biblical affirmation that he is created in the image of God. He has the power of self-determination, to make decisions, to change, to envision the future that God is creating, and to enter into new relationships with God and his fellowmen. It is as if God were peering over the shoulder of man into a pool of water and seeing a reflection of some of his own powers embodied in him. This reflection depends upon man's being in right relationship to God. It is distorted when man takes over the running of life, ignores his responsibilities, or seeks to escape from this true relationship to God by lapsing into sensuality. If we can assume that man has come of age today and has the power to manage life, then Christians must keep clear their relationship to God. Jesus Christ acted to reconcile man to God so that he might not have to live overwhelmed by fear, guilt, and dread of the future. This is the personal history of each Christian. He identifies himself with it. If man will accept the fact that God accepts him and will enter into right relations with him, he can be a new person capable of making new starts in life. Living by this faith, life opens new possibilities. He lives in God's time wherein God fulfills what his finite limitations leave uncompleted.

The Christian participates in history by sharing this interpretation with his fellowmen. By helping laymen in the decision-making councils rediscover their relationship to God as their creator and redeemer, he helps them to enter the processes that are life-sustaining, not deadly and destroying. The Christian can accept persons who basically differ from him because he knows that God accepts them. The Christian can support the forces that are working redemptively to serve people of other lands to bring about the conditions wherein God's new age can be realized. He can accept the partial realization of God's purposes in our time. As he becomes aware of his limitations and finiteness, he places deeper trust in God and rediscovers the relationship that renews him in spirit and guides his destiny.

UNDERSTANDING THE BIBLICAL VIEW OF HISTORY

Contemporary Christians are confused continuously by the ideological warfare of secular forces and the partial, obscurantist view of church traditions. Such a view is usually built on one verse or one book of the Bible. Christian laymen need an acquaintance with a more inclusive interpretation of history if they are going to be an effective influence upon modern man. At least eight basic biblical perspectives of history need to be understood as guidelines to a comprehensive view of history. Christian laymen who seek in freedom to apply them to life individually and collectively will gain a sense of direction, overcome confusion based on too narrow a view, and find deliverance from their present state of anxiety.

1. The Bible teaches us that God is the ruler of history. This recurrent theme was expressed in the early days when the tribes of Israel were forming a nation. It was reechoed in the voices of the prophets, and it was sung in the Psalms after the Exile. "God is the king of all the earth" (Ps. 47:7).

2. The foundations of society are built upon moral law. Moses led the people of Israel into an awareness of this moral obligation and the necessity of accepting it, were they to survive as a nation. It was the prophets who held up the plumb line and called the people of Israel to keep building the nation on the basis of this moral law. And when this covenant-keeping people had broken the law and its social obligations, it was Jeremiah who tried to elicit an inner motive that would prompt the people to live by the spirit of the law rather than coerced by outward forms of restraint, whether these forms came from statesman or priest. Jeremiah said, "Behold, the days are coming, says the Lord, when I will make a new covenant with the house of Israel and the house of Judah . . . . I will put my law within them, and I will write it upon their hearts; and I will be their God, and they shall be my people. . . . for I will forgive their

iniquity, and I will remember their sin no more" (Jer. 31:31-34). The philosopher Karl Jaspers applies this affirmation of biblical faith to contemporary life:

God may want man to live and survive in the world, but not unconditionally. . . . We may think, in the symbolism of the divine will, that God has not told man to destroy himself but has given him a choice in time: survival, on condition of changing into a better man, or doom. The redemption from atomic death cannot succeed if everything else about man remains as before.[4]

3. God can use the enemies of a people to awaken it to new moral insights and to prompt it to new spiritual relationships. Isaiah pointed to the persecuting Assyrians as "the rod of God's anger." Jeremiah called Nebuchadnezzar "the servant of God who would serve until his own time should come." Isaiah looked upon Cyrus and the persecuting Persians as "the anointed for a function." This is the same principle that is implied in the saying that "the bee that stings the flower also pollenates it." It was the observation of Romain Rolland after World War I that the world might have become a unity but that mankind was not yet fit for this high destiny. Perhaps through this biblical principle we see that part of the ambiguity and breakdown in our time is a stimulus to more inclusive moral and spiritual unities that want to emerge.

4. The Bible tells us that history moves toward an end not simply chronologically but purposefully, toward a *telos* (goal). There is a fundamental difference here between Greek and Hebrew thoughts. Greek thought looked upon history as a cycle in which there was birth, growth, decay and rebirth. Hebrew thought looked upon history as moving toward the working out of God's plan and purpose among men. It was that far-off divine event toward which the whole creation moved. This

[4] *The Future of Mankind,* p. 255.

idea Jesus took over when he said that the consummation of human history is the kingdom of God. This truth needs to be asserted by Christians with a new firm faith so that people and leaders of our time may become aware that we live our lives in the presence of an eternal order in history and that the end of time is the fulfillment of God's purpose, not the destruction of man and nature.

5. Although we are pushed by our anxieties because our life is transitory, we must recapture the New Testament teaching that God is eternal. "In the fullness of time" God sent forth his Son. Since that time the destiny of man has been different. Through that act God revealed to man what he was like. What men had understood only as *words* prior to that moment became *flesh* and dwelt among them. It was the advent of a new era. Through their inner personal relationship with Jesus, men discovered again the image of God. This image became the guiding image of their lives; it filled their days with hope and meaning.

This sense of time in which God fulfills his purpose in history can be either creative or destructive. The church has experienced both in its history. It depends upon human response as well as many unknown dynamic forces in any new and emerging situation. In his volume, *Human Destiny*, Lecomte du Noüy has warned,

"Let every man remember that the destiny of mankind is incomparable and that it depends greatly on his will to collaborate in the transcendent task. Let Man remember that the law is and always has been to struggle and that the fight has lost nothing of its violence by being transposed from the material onto the spiritual plane. Let him remember that his own dignity, his nobility as a human being must emerge from his efforts to liberate himself from his bondage and to obey his deepest aspirations. And let him above all never forget that the divine spark is in him, in him alone, and that he is free to disregard it, to kill it, or to come closer to God by showing his eagerness to work with him and for him." [5]

6. When the Word became flesh and dwelt among us, a new dialogue between man and God began that has affected the whole panorama of history ever since. Mankind can discover the will of God as Jesus has made it known and implement it in human history in the relationships of man with other men. The central fact of the gospel is this: God has done something. He has entered human history, Jesus is here. This is the turning point of history and we still live in the year of our Lord—in the time when his Spirit and his way of life are made known to men. In him the old order has ended and a new order has begun.

George Buttrick pointed to this situation with clarity when he said, "History is dialogue between God and man-in-pilgrimage in the language of Event; and Christ is the conversation's middle term, the key to the translation, the light in which the whole pilgrimage can be seen and understood, and the love in which history's brokenness is healed." [6]

7. Along with the apostle Paul we must recognize that God was in Christ, reconciling the world unto himself. Whenever men get messed up in their own feelings and relationships, whenever society and nations get enmeshed in conflict, they are not hopelessly caught in a web of destructive forces of evil that lead them to blind fury of destruction. Christ met all the destructive forces of evil, both personal and social; he met selfishness, greed, power, lust, jealousy, hatred, and vengeance and yet he walked right through this maze on to the cross. Through suffering, he reconciled his people to God, saying, "Father, into thy hands I commit my Spirit." This fact enables us to come before God and be reconciled to him. As John Bright says in his

[5] P. 275.
[6] *Christ and History*, p. 44.

book, *The Kingdom of God*, "Exactly here is the relationship of social gospel to the gospel of individual salvation, and it is important that we get it. The two are not to be set apart as has so often been done, for they are two aspects of the same thing." [7] The Christian religion is both a moral demand and an offer of salvation. This is the clue to history. This Christian truth enables us to rise with faith above the tragedies of our time and to work with freedom from fear for a future which God shall fulfill. The end of man's history does not need to be complete destruction of man and nature but reconciliation with the Eternal.

8. During the persecution of the Christians by Domitian, the author of the book of Revelation wrote a symbolic interpretation of history to show that the forces of evil never overcome God. His thesis was that God has already had a victory in heaven, that Michael and his angels have cast down the old serpent from heaven. (Rev. 12:7-10.) This is based on an Iranian myth. It was given as the reason why the forces of evil are so vicious on the earth. The Christians are to be faithful and believe that God will give them the victory. This philosophy broke the Greek concept of history and its cycle of fate—birth, growth, decay, rebirth.

Oswald Spengler revived this cyclical view in our time, and Reinhold Niebuhr comments, "It cannot be denied that, since the freedom of history rises on the ground of nature-necessity, historical destiny is always partly determined by the vitality and decay of the natural forces underlying any historical achievement." [8] However, he further observes that each civilization usually makes some choice promoted by pride, desire for power, repression, imperialism, or the use of old strategies in new situations where they do not apply.

As science and the new technology bring nations and civiliza-

[7] P. 223.
[8] *The Nature and Destiny of Man*, II, 303.

tions of the world closer together through speed of travel and communication, the possibilities both for greater unity and conflicts are enhanced. There is nothing inevitable about the outcome of our history. It is the arena in which we are called to match our beliefs concerning the meaning and end of history against the heinous destructive forces at work in the intergroup and international relations of our time. While working for peace, justice, and the kind of unity that is supported by and fulfilled in God's realm and God's time, we may be saved from those premature realizations in time and the predisposed inclinations toward setting up our little domains of power. From this perspective we can see that there is partial realization of human action in history, judgment upon the evil in the forms of life, society, and institutions we devise, reformation and fulfillment of life in the end that God consumates. Alpha and Omega—these symbols are the ultimate ground of our hope.

In the light of this biblical perspective, the laity—the people of God—are summoned to bring their understanding of destiny of mankind as the fulfillment of the intention of God to bear upon the issues and decisions that make our history.

Participating in a Meaningful History

Deep within himself, man senses that he is destined for a meaningful existence, yet he feels overwhelmed by gigantic impersonal forces around him. The world is run by specialists. He yearns to be a part of the history-making events of his time. If history is the arena wherein the salvation of man is being wrought out now and wherein the directions of the future are being chosen, the laity seek to find the meaning of their lives as they relate the spiritual and moral forces to the forces of necessity and expediency, which all too frequently become the determiners of destiny.

The Hebrews were called to bring mankind to an awareness of the moral law; the Greeks brought perceptions of beauty;

the Romans obedience to civil law; the Renaissance new learning; the Germans the life of faith; the English industrialism
and the manufacture of things; the Indians serenity through
contemplation. And to what is mankind called today? By virtue
of new health, longer life, increased learning, the unleashing of
unlimited power, the discovery of satellite communication, and
jet-speed of travel, man is called to the re-creation of new forms
of unity wherein all the streams of the past may be pooled into
new life-sustaining forms. It is up to the Christian to create an
awareness of the meaning of the events that confront him in the
light of the gospel. Above all, it is to "be there." The Negro
spiritual, "Were you there when they crucified my Lord?" expresses it cogently. In the laboratories, the market place, the
council tables, the hospital rooms, Christians must "be there" as
authentic representatives of God's new age that is coming into
being.

If people are going to be motivated to live as Christians and
to fulfill their destinies in the world, they will have to be stirred
in the spiritual depths of their beings. Education for churchmanship in the world must go deeper than passing opinions about
the Bible or reciting historical facts about Jesus. These will not
be enough to enable adults to identify themselves with Christ
and his church. Christians must be aware of what God is doing
where the decisions are being made. Christ is Lord of the whole
church. Therefore laymen must become involved in the church
universal and find creative ways for the church universal to bring
new unity into the world. Motivation for this kind of churchmanship comes as response, in the depths of their souls, to the
love of God and to the work which Christ is doing for them.
Unless churchmen can manifest in history the churches' unity
that is in Christ, they cannot contribute much to the history of
their times.

Education for churchmanship that is relevant to man's destiny
cannot be a monologue. God who disclosed himself to man and

sent the Holy Spirit to lead the church continually into truth and power is present in the life of the world today. As leaders seek to help people know God in all his redeeming, loving, and creative power, they must be cocreators. This creativeness must confront the barriers that divide men into hostile camps. It must enable persons in freedom to surmount these barriers. It calls for the creation of a new living dialogue among laymen of all races, nations, and religions. It summons adults to adventure in lifetime learning in which the purpose of God is being discovered in a whole new set of relationships. It beckons laymen all over the world to open doors to people so they may participate more widely not only in the material benefits of civilization and culture but also in the spiritual and intellectual ones.

When Peter discovered through his daily contacts with Jesus that he was the Messiah, he changed through a series of testing experiences to a new way of believing and a new way of understanding life. As adults learn more of the Christian way of life through personal relationships with those who are mature churchmen, they may become a part of the mission of Christ's working force on earth. This means that we must develop new disciplines in our interpersonal relationships. In a world come of age, the old distinctions of superior and inferior people will not hold. We must learn how to listen to the hurts of the world and to respond with integrity to the inner spirit of other men. For some Christians it means participation in the suffering of the world because this is the discipleship to which Christ calls them. In so doing, they may become part of a new humanity that is seeking to overcome some of the self-centeredness of their "ego-centered" religion and to find spiritual resources for a reorientation of their own lives. As participants they renew their discipleship and seek the word of hope, the word of love, the word of compassion that they may be agents of reconciliation to their fellowmen who have become alienated from God. Christians who are in the process of changing can be the purveyors of change in the lives of other people who then become a force for altering the course of history. They can enable them to face the future with hope.

Mankind stands today at the brink of total destruction or the beginning of a new age of world history. Christians view any emerging era from the perspective of God's creative and providential action in history, his self-disclosure in Jesus Christ whose redemptive action in the fullness of time initiated a new dynamic existence for man, and in the light of the kingdom of God as the end of history. The Christian response is in faith that impels participation in history in the full knowledge that all past ages were mixtures of good and evil and that the age to come will bring only partial realization of God's realm in history. It is in our personal choices that God confronts us with his realm of meanings, values, and relationships. It is in our decisions about the future that Christ comes again and again to clarify and to judge the ends we seek. To those who respond to the grace of God, Christ comes into our history again to influence it.

As Christians seek to realize new forms of unity among the churches and the nations, they must become vividly aware that such unity is real now in the realm of God. In the realm of nature, the accumulated forces of social evil are potent factors causing fragmentation. Wholeness, health, unity are gifts to us of the holiness of God. By participating in the life of faith, we receive them and cause others to be aware of them in the world. So long as churches insist upon unity in their own images, they create dissension and increase the fragmentation of the world. As soon as laymen move out from the church gathered in the world, they are the church ecumenical—the unity of God's realm. They may participate in this unity as they seek that kind of health, wholeness, understanding, and brotherhood which embodies an inclusive, apostolic mission in the world. Trusting in the Holy Spirit to make them sensitive and alert, in Jesus Christ as Lord to give them power and wisdom, and in God to fulfill in his time what is realized only partially, they may seek with openness and outgoing service to be the church universal whose faith embodied can make men whole again.

Chapter 10
Bibliography

Bright, John. *The Kingdom of God*. Nashville: Abingdon Press, 1953.

Buttrick, George. *Christ and History*. Nashville: Abingdon Press, 1963.

Cox, H., *The Secular City*, New York: Macmillan, 1965.

Cullman, Oscar. *Christ and Time*. Philadelphia: Westminster Press, 1950.

de Chardin, Teilhard, Pierre. *The Phenomenon of Man*. New York: Harper, 1961.

du Noüy, Lecomte. *Human Destiny*. New York: New American Library, Mentor. Longmans, 1947.

Jaspers, Karl. *The Future of Mankind*. Chicago: University of Chicago Press, 1961.

Marney, Carlyle. *These Things Remain*. Nashville: Abingdon Press, 1953.

Miller, Arthur. *The Crucible*. New York: Viking Press, 1964.

———. *Death of a Salesman*. New York: Viking Press, 1949.

Niebuhr, Reinhold. *The Nature and Destiny of Man*. New York: Scribners, 1943.

Osborn, R. E. *A Church for These Times*. Nashville: Abingdon Press, 1965.

St. Augustine. *The City of God*. New York: The Modern Library, 1950.

Tillich, Paul, *Systematic Theology*, 3 vols. Chicago: University of Chicago Press, 1951, 1957, 1963.

Toynbee, Arnold. *A Study of History*. ed. D. C. Somervell. 2 vols. New York: Oxford University Press, 1947, 1957.

Williams, Tennessee. *The Glass Menagerie*. New York: New Directions.

————. *A Streetcar Named Desire*. New York: New Directions, 1947.

Winter, Gibson. *The New Creation as Metropolis*. New York: Macmillan, 1963.

INDEX OF SCRIPTURE

INDEX OF SUBJECTS

Groups
  communication in, 119-20
  participation in learning, 50-52
  responsible participation, 115-
    19
Grünewald, Matthias, 38

Hahn, Otto, 182
Handel, George Frederick, 38
Harkness, Georgia, 25
Heidegger, Martin, 155
Heisenberg, 183
Hiroshima, 182
History, 191
  biblical perspectives upon, 186
  Christian interpretation of, 183
  God's purpose in, 185
History-making, 191
Hollister, W. H., 126
Holy Spirit, 24, 40, 48, 51, 55,
    70, 78, 92, 104, 193, 194
"House churches," 128
Human Destiny, 188
Hutterite brethren, 40

Image
  of contemporary man, 184
  of churchmanship, 15
  of self, 29, 30
Isaiah, 187

James and John, 107
Jaspers, Karl, 187
Jerusalem, Upper Room, 20
Jesus Christ
  as Messiah, 193
  in history, 183
  Lord of history, 189
  resurrection, 20

Joshua, 20
Julian, 34, 35, 156, 173

Kingdom of God, the, 190
Kafka, Franz, 169
Kraemer, H., 24
Krutch, J. W., 81

Laity
  act of remembrance, 49
  and history making, 37-39,
    191-95
  potential of, 30, 31
  response to gospel, 46-49
  servanthood of, 54, 55
  unfrozen, 24
  views of, 28, 29
"Laos," 48
Laymen, 22, 23, 24
  church view of, 28, 29
  corporate demonstration, 49
  forms of transformation, 125-
    27
  images of, 44, 45
  in dialogue in the world, 50,
    51
  in early church, 32
  in Reformation, 37
  religious life in Middle Ages,
    35
  response to gospel, 48
Leadership
  cost of, 107-9
  described, 104-7
  experiment in shared, 115-19
  functions of, 107-9, 112-15
  style of, 110-12
Learning, approaches to, 87-100
Lecturing, 87, 88, 89